STRAIGHT No CHASER

SOUND BITES

STRAIGHT No CHASER
SOUND BITES

A CAPPELLA, COCKTAILS, AND CUISINE

STRAIGHT NO CHASER, INC.

RED LIGHTNING BOOKS

This book is a publication of

Red Lightning Books
1320 East 10th Street
Bloomington, Indiana 47405 USA

Redlightningbooks.com

Manufactured in the United States of America

Library of Congress Cataloging-in-Publication Data

Names: Straight No Chaser (Musical group) author.
Title: Straight No Chaser sound bites : a cappella,
    cocktails, and cuisine / Straight No Chaser, Inc.
Description: Bloomington : Red Lightning Books, 2021.
Identifiers: LCCN 2021038082 (print) | LCCN 2021038083 (ebook) |
    ISBN 9781684351725 (hardback) | ISBN 9781684351732 (ebook)
Subjects: LCSH: Straight No Chaser (Musical group) | Vocal groups—
    United States. | Cookbooks. | Cocktails. | LCGFT: Cookbooks.
Classification: LCC ML421.S8165 S77 2021 (print) | LCC
    ML421.S8165 (ebook) | DDC 782.806—dc23
LC record available at https://lccn.loc.gov/2021038082
LC ebook record available at https://lccn.loc.gov/2021038083

First Printing 2021

To our families, who have instilled in us
a love of music and food.

To our fans, the Chasers, who allowed us a career in music.

And to our fellow creators: whether it's pastries or performance,
we hope this fuels your inspiration.

CONTENTS

FOREWORD

The story of Straight No Chaser is a story of luck, timing, and talent. But most importantly, it's about second chances in life. Little did I know that, on New Year's Day 2008, I would discover a group that would be one of the most unique signings I've made in my career. On that fateful day, I was surfing YouTube when I came across a video of an all-male collegiate a cappella group performing a unique version of "The 12 Days of Christmas." I was instantly captivated. It was natural, uncontrived, and all the growth—a phenomenal eight million views at that point—was totally organic.

That same morning, I called Randy. At first, he thought it was some kind of prank, but I managed to convince him otherwise and flew Randy Stine and Dan Ponce to LA. We met over dinner, and I suggested that the group come to New York for a live audition before the Atlantic team later that month. But that proved far easier said than done. As it turned out, the video I had watched was over nine years old, and the band members had long since graduated and dispersed into the real world of families and jobs, mostly outside of music and entertainment. To compound the situation, they were scattered across the globe.

Nevertheless, I offered to fly them all in from wherever they were. Happily, they agreed. Outside of a wedding here and there, this was the first time they had sung together in a decade. They were incredible, and I got a deal in motion that same day. I just had a feeling about these guys. Some people in the office were surprised by my decision, and some, I found out later, even thought it was a joke. To me, however, this was very serious business. I believed if we could take the passion people have for collegiate a cappella and give the group a platform on the world stage, it could really happen for them.

I decided I could risk one hundred thousand dollars on what was admittedly a long shot—fifty thousand to make an album and fifty thousand to the band members, which came out to a mere five thousand each. On top of that, I told them that the only way this was going to work would be if they quit their successful day jobs so they could go on the road, and people could hear and see them in person. It was, of course, a preposterous suggestion, but the guys went back to their families and everyone miraculously agreed that yes, it was crazy, and yes, they would go for it. Needless to say, I was thrilled.

We moved quickly to get Straight No Chaser into the studio to record their first Atlantic album, *Holiday Spirits*, and we were feeling good about our chances. We released the album at the end of October 2008 and . . . nothing. We couldn't get any traction, and I felt terrible, thinking that I'd ruined these guys' lives. They had to go back to their families and have very hard conversations about their future. They had quit their jobs to follow their passion and their dream, and now what?

Meanwhile, however, the Atlantic team hadn't given up. They landed SNC some key holiday TV bookings, including a game-changing appearance on the *Today Show* on December 22. The reaction was phenomenal. The album instantly went from nowhere to number one on the iTunes and Amazon charts, and the group landed major press in the likes of the *New York Times*. The demand for live bookings exploded, and they went from singing in hotel piano bars to major concert venues. And *Holiday Spirits* became their first gold album.

Straight No Chaser took off at a time of huge uncertainty, in the midst of the great market crash and recession of 2008. Conventional wisdom would have said it wasn't the best moment to release new music from an unproven, non-traditional artist. But, against all odds, SNC's story resonated during a moment in history when people just wanted a little hope. They were the perfect antidote to all the bad news in the world. It was a story for the ages: a group of guys who had long given up on their dream of musical success being given a second chance and rising to the occasion.

Over the years, we've recorded and released many records together, shared many meals, and enjoyed lots of conversations. One of the rewards of being a music exec is to build long-term relationships with successful artists, and this has been one of my most unexpected and special experiences. SNC has recorded with Sir Paul McCartney, Sir Elton John, Phil Collins, Dolly Parton, and many more. Seeing what has happened since that New Year's Day in 2008 fills me with a true sense of pride at all that they've accomplished.

I hope the Straight No Chaser story is shared across many tables over many meals. For me, the moral is that very rarely in life do you get a second chance at your dream, so if it comes your way, take it. It's never too late to pursue something you love.

Craig Kallman
Chairman and CEO, Atlantic Records

ACKNOWLEDGMENTS

Straight No Chaser would like to thank our writer Claire Krawsczyn, and Emily Morgan for introducing us; David Hulsey, Stephen Williams, Darja Malcolm-Clarke, Anna Francis, Jennifer Witzke, and Tony Brewer at Indiana University Press; Josh Adams; Evan DeStefano; Jimmy Fontaine; Vincent Holloway; Craig Kallman at Atlantic Records; Kevin Gore at Arts Music; David Britz, Ben Haley, Luke Pierce, Kyle Novak, Constance Torres, and Jessie Chambers at WORKS Entertainment; Andrea Johnson, Claire Greising, Scott Mantell, and Steve Levine at ICM Partners; David Roberts; Ashley White; Lauren Phillips; Tara Nichols; Mike Taylor; Bob Rager; Jonin Fehlmann; Dan Schultz; Dan Donaldson; Joe Wine; Rick Dixon; Indiana University, and the Indiana University Alumni Association; Ryan Ahlwardt, Mike Itkoff, Don Nottingham, Dan Ponce, and all SNC and Another Round members past and present; the millions of YouTube viewers who made this possible; and most importantly, our wives and children: Molly, Kristen, Jamie, Zoë, Julia, Emily, Kate, Lindsey, Lauryn, Sam, James, Aaliyah, Bryson, Leo, Mila, Nova, Ivy, Hayden, Eli, Lily, Will, Callan, Henry, Theo, and Carly, and all our friends and family.

Straight No Chaser

Sound Bites

Straight No Chaser began at Indiana University in 1996, and all past and present group members are IU graduates. They return to the Bloomington campus to visit as a group as often as possible.
Credit: Evan De Stefano Photography

SOUND BITES

AN INTRODUCTION

David "DR" Roberts

A cappella and food. What's the connection? As a former member of Straight No Chaser, and its current business manager, allow me to set the stage, and the table. We would like to share some more of what's made us who we are, literally and figuratively: our favorite recipes and stories. Recipes are not simply words on a card, screen, or book. They represent time shared with friends and family. Because cooking, like singing, is more fun together.

Straight No Chaser was born in the autumn of 1996 at Indiana University. We rehearsed at least three times a week and performed at every opportunity we could: dorms, cafeterias, sorority houses, alumni receptions, and restaurants of all kinds. Generally, if food or girls were involved—ideally both—we were there. I still remember our first rehearsal after a winter break. As we finished singing a Boyz-II-Men song, Jerome looked around and gave voice to what we were all thinking: "Man, I missed you guys."

We just loved singing together. And after a few hundred rehearsals and performances, and dozens of road trips to perform at rival colleges and a cappella competitions, we also enjoyed eating together. Part of any great college experience is exploring the best local food stops. We have our favorites: Kilroy's on Kirkwood, Nick's English Hut, Upland Brewing, Yogi's Bar & Grill, Lennie's, Laughing Planet Cafe, Dragon Express, the Uptown Cafe, Malibu Grill, Mother Bear's Pizza, Pizza X, the Trojan Horse, Dagwood's Sandwiches, and of course Janko's Little Zagreb. To this day, our trips to Bloomington revolve around some of these spots. Which is to say that our visits include way too much food in far too little time.

While we love our old haunts, restaurants aren't actually our favorite food stops. Whether you're a poor college kid or a musician on tour, there's nothing

Straight No Chaser performs "Creep" by Radiohead in Napa Valley, California, July 2018.
Credit: Josh Adams

like home cooking. All of our parents have at some time or another cooked for the group, and we've gotten to know each other's family favorites. A prime example of this is Mr. Stine's famous grilled beef tenderloin, which punctuated summer gigs in Chicago. Or Mom Luginbill's slider sandwiches, which are an essential tour bus snack. Then we have the Mechlings' green bean casserole, a welcome leftover post-Thanksgiving. Mrs. Shilanskas' Italian sausage pasta is the basis for my own pasta dish, though hers is demonstrably better. The Morgans' sugar pie is a rare treat given that Steve almost never leaves food on the table. I'm not going to say we fight over Mrs. Trepp's Buffalo chicken dip, but demand definitely exceeds supply anytime the tour rolls through Iowa. Mrs. Isho's biryani is so good you'll eat too much and sleep through the second half of the game (true story). My family's toffee bars originated with my Aunt Judy, but it was my grandmother ("Suki" to her eight grandkids) who gave life to the holiday tradition.

Which brings us to our all-time, hands-down favorite meal: Jerome's mother's fried chicken and her caramel cake. The latter of which is a recipe Mrs. Collins has closely guarded for years. I am beyond excited that she has finally shared this invaluable family secret.

Food, has always been a major theme of our gatherings. So much so that it occasionally turned into a sport, for example, seeing who could eat the most wings, or at a Brazilian steakhouse, who would be the last to turn his card to red. To the best of my knowledge and research, Steve was involved in all of these food-related competitions and remains undefeated to this day.

When we began touring, our love of food went on the road. Here again, we've had the incredible opportunity to enjoy some of the best food across our great country. And believe me when I say that we took full advantage: Emmy Squared, Whiskey Kitchen, Slider Haus, and Saint Stephen in Nashville; Heavenly and Basalt in Honolulu; Gibsons, LUXBAR, and Au Cheval in Chicago; Miso Phat and Monkeypod on Maui; Sushi Den and Pho 16th in Denver; Pirates Den, Laguna Grill, and Back Bay in Brigantine;

TOFFEE BARS

Dessert, Snack, Breakfast

SERVES THE FAMILY AND THEN SOME

PREP: 20 MINUTES   **COOK: 30 MINUTES**

INGREDIENTS

1 cup brown sugar

1 cup sugar

¾ cup shortening

¾ cup butter

2 teaspoons vanilla

1 teaspoon salt

4 eggs

2 cups flour, sifted

2 cups uncooked rolled oats

2 pkgs semisweet chocolate chips

Heat oven to 350°F.

Cream sugar, shortening, and butter together. Mix in vanilla, salt, and eggs. Add flour and rolled oats. Mix.

Pour into a greased 13 × 9 inch baking pan. Bake for 20–30 minutes (do not overbake).

Separately, melt chocolate chips in a double boiler. Spread melted chocolate over bars while still hot from oven. Allow chocolate to cool and cut into bars.

Doug Fir Lounge at the Jupiter Hotel and Mother's Cafe in Portland, Oregon; Terry Black's and Franklin BBQ in Austin; Bern's in Tampa; River House in Portsmouth, Maine; Nuevo Laredo in Atlanta; Legal Seafood in Boston; Frank Pepe at Mohegan Sun in Uncasville; Rendezvous and Moe's Original BBQ in Memphis; St. Elmo in Indianapolis; Tin Roof in LA; Matt's Bar in Minneapolis; Ozumo in San Francisco; Lenny's in NYC; Q39 in Kansas City; Butcher and Singer in Philadelphia; Anchor Bar in Buffalo; and Duke's in DC, to name a few. Not to mention the countless amazing catering operations we've enjoyed throughout the years and across the country. Our rider states: "If there's a local specialty, please include that as an option."

Straight No Chaser grew out of a shared love of music, each of us, like a great recipe, adding something unique to make a more interesting whole. After twenty-five years of making music and meals together, we are much more than what you see on stage. One of the few constants in our lives has been this group, the music we've created and shared, and the food we've enjoyed together. Now, we want to share all of that with you. It's our way of saying "thank you" for allowing Straight No Chaser to be part of your family. So kick back, have a drink, put on your favorite SNC album, and explore the joys of cooking for and with your friends and family.

The group answers questions during a meet and greet at
their sound check at the IU Auditorium, December 2019.
Credit: Evan De Stefano Photography

VERSE 1

JEROME COLLINS

There's No Stopping the Split

Jerome Collins is an avid entertainer. He holds the Straight No Chaser record for splitting his pants, and he's proud of it. Ever since he was a cheeky toddler humming Motown hits in his childhood home in Allentown, Pennsylvania, Jerome has been putting on shows for friends and family. His persona has always been huge: big personality, strong voice, and major dance moves.

Jerome took his cues from his family—everyone knows Papa Collins's booming voice when he's in the audience—and his musical idols. During the 1983 special *Motown 25: Yesterday, Today, Forever*, Jerome was glued to the television screen as Michael Jackson performed the moonwalk for the first time on air. The bright lights and big stage made sense to Jerome. He started working on his own routines at home, practicing the moves that would get him the performance impact that he wanted. The splits were an obvious choice: they were fun to do, added a little element of surprise, and could punctuate the perfect on-stage moment. He practiced them—sometimes just for fun, as kids do—and sometimes to bring home his performance.

Jerome bringing his passion for performance to the stage.
Credit: Evan De Stefano Photography

SN-TINI

Cocktail

First created for Gibsons Steakhouse, Jerome created his own version of a Straight No Chaser Martini, known affectionately as the SN-tini.

INGREDIENTS

1 can of Pellegrino Blood Orange

2 shots of vodka

1 chilled glass

3–4 jalapenos

Gibsons Seasoning Salt

———————————————

Fill mixer jar with ice.

Wet the lip of chilled glass and roll the rim in Gibsons Seasoning Salt.

Muddle 3–4 seeded jalapenos; strain; and drain the juice into mixer jar. Add vodka and Pellegrino to mixer jar. Shake vigorously to combine.

Pour into chilled glass and serve with a slice of jalapeno on the side.

SNC High Note: Rim your glass with coarse salt like a margarita, and top with a small wedge of grapefruit if you're feeling fancy.

Jerome loves to perform, even during rehearsals.
Credit: Evan De Stefano Photography

Forty-something years later, Jerome is still doing the splits on stage. Typically, it goes well; Jerome drops into a split, the audience roars, and the energy is maxed out for a blissful moment before the next beat drops. But, inevitably, there are those *other* occasions when an on-stage split gets a little . . . loose. Literally. As in splitting his pants wide open on stage in front of thousands of people kind of loose.

Jerome can recall five times that he's split his pants on stage. The collective mind of the fans (known as Chasers) can probably recall each of them, too. Jerome will never forget the breeze he felt the first time it happened in 2011. Straight No Chaser was in the middle of doing their mash-up of "Billie Jean" and "Poison." It's a particularly good song for Jerome, who often gets to channel his childhood icon and don Michael Jackson's signature getup. At the end of one of his solo parts, Jerome drops into a split to mark the transition. As Jerome went down, his pants went wide at the seam. He made a face, which was quickly noted by the other guys on stage. In a split second, Jerome had to decide what to do from there. The options were to either try to go on and work with split pants on stage, or to try to manage a graceful exit from the stage to fix the situation.

The size of the split pretty much made his decision for him. Jerome laughed, gave a modest-yet-fun peek of the split to the audience, and stepped off stage to get patched up. The staff and crew weren't as accustomed to the world of Jerome's split pants yet. The best solution was a perilous combination of paper clips and staples. Jerome made it work, got back on stage, and finished the show.

Even if a split isn't part of the practiced choreography, it's not unlikely for Jerome to drop into the splits at some point during a performance. After the first public split, they reinforced the seams of Jerome's pants, carried sewing kits in their wardrobe cases, and even kept extra pairs of pants offstage. Finally, knowing it would be more family-friendly and hassle-free if his pants could withstand the exuberance, Straight No Chaser switched to wearing high-end athletic pants on stage with their suits and ties.

The group is fully onboard with the signature Jerome Collins onstage split. As Tyler Trepp once said, "We don't know what's going to happen in a show, but there's a really good chance that Jerome will split his pants." As Jerome stated, "My pants need to be able to keep up!" (pun intended). There's just no stopping the spirit of the split.

MOMMA C'S FRIED CHICKEN

Main Course

SERVES 4

This is a classic fried chicken recipe, and Jerome insists it tastes better when prepared with a little Momma Collins magic and a side of patience.

PREP: 20 MINUTES   **COOK: 40 MINUTES**

INGREDIENTS

1 ½ cups milk

2 large eggs

2 ½ cups all-purpose flour

2 tablespoons salt (plus additional for sprinkling)

2 teaspoons black pepper

3 pounds chicken (bone-in, skin-on pieces)

1 cup Crisco

Combine milk and eggs in a large bowl.

Pour flour onto a plate, or dump it into a bag for shaking.

Salt chicken by sprinkling salt on both sides of each piece.

Roll the chicken in the milk and eggs, then dip or shake chicken in flour until fully covered.

Heat Crisco in a 12-inch cast-iron skillet until it reaches a temperature of 365°F. Fry coated chicken uncovered until brown on bottom, about 10–15 minutes. Add pepper to each chicken piece while it is frying. Turn each piece over to fry the opposite side. Sprinkle with pepper.

Monitor chicken closely to avoid burning; each piece should cook for 20–24 minutes total. Chicken is ready when internal temperature reaches 170°.

Remove from skillet and place on paper towel to drain grease. Serve and enjoy!

SNC High Note: Love fried chicken? Great! There's another recipe in Randy's chapter from Chef Art Smith. Fried chicken for everyone!

The Barry Manilow Ego Check

There are dozens of Straight No Chaser experiences that carry lifelong lessons with them. Straight No Chaser started as a collegiate group at Indiana University. The roots of the group were built like a very talented fraternity. After being signed to Atlantic Records in 2008, there was a lot of professional growth for each member of Straight No Chaser and for the group as a whole. Jerome has a vivid memory of one of the most affecting and significant lessons of his musical careers, served up by none other than the legendary Barry Manilow.

In 2010, Straight No Chaser collaborated with Barry Manilow, recording his song "One Voice" for their album *With a Twist*. In May 2011, Straight No Chaser was invited to open for Barry Manilow, at the O2 Arena in London. With a capacity of twenty-thousand people, this was a huge opportunity for the guys to win over new fans. Jerome recalls the overall experience being surreal, but not without its challenges. In Jerome's experience, working with Manilow was a prime chance to get his ego checked. Manilow was an incredibly talented and disciplined musician and performer. Jerome observed how Manilow was intimately involved in every aspect of his shows, because he seemed to want to create a very specific experience for his audience. Jerome recalls the group's last-minute efforts to learn a few of Manilow's arrangements for the encore, blend in with Manilow's show, and even take cues from him about how they stood together for pictures. It was challenging, but absolutely worth it for Jerome, who reveled in the opportunity to learn from a tried-and-true star. Jerome realized that there's no time or threshold in a performer's life when suddenly the experience and the fans take a back seat: even someone with a history as long and storied as Manilow's required diligence and perseverance to enact year after year. Jerome realized that while it's not the only path to success and creating a true brand as a performer, there are many musicians who work constantly to create exactly what they want out of their careers.

The lessons of observing and watching Manilow was inspiring, while receiving his feedback, adjustments, and precise instructions was a

As the guys perform outdoors at Wolf Trap National Park in Vienna, Virginia, Jerome appears on the big screen. *Credit: Josh Adams*

challenge. It was all worthwhile. The result was a Barry Manilow–approved performance and roaring applause from twenty thousand new fans.

Drop It Like It's Hot

Wolf Trap National Park for the Performing Arts is the nation's only national park dedicated to performance. In addition to walking paths and hiking trails, the park is home to several theaters, amphitheaters, and stages that host hundreds of performances each year. Peak season is the summer months, when long days and warm weather bring thousands of fans to Wolf Trap for performances from their favorite groups, including Straight No Chaser. On a hot Sunday in August 2012, Straight No Chaser was preparing to take the stage. Vienna, Virginia, where Wolf Trap is located, doesn't escape the sweltering heat that plagues nearby Washington, DC, during its notoriously swampy summer months. Outdoor performances can be a challenge in any situation because of the unpredictability of the weather, but Straight No Chaser was used to adapting to their surroundings. They double down on water, wear a lighter wardrobe, and simply deal with sweat running down their faces while they sing. It's a part of being a performer.

On this particular day, Jerome had a new and different complexity to manage. He was fighting a cold, and Jerome is a self-identified baby when it comes to handling illnesses, particularly while touring. He's known for hitting preventative measures hard if he senses any sort of illness creeping in: he'll up his vitamin intake, pop Benadryl and Mucinex, drink hot tea—anything to keep his health optimum and his voice at its prime. As he prepared for the Wolf Trap performance, Jerome knew he wasn't at peak performance status. His cold was worse before the show than it was earlier in the day. He turned to all of his regular antidotes to make it through the performance, including a piping hot cup of tea before walking onto the stage on a sweltering day.

Straight No Chaser started the set with "Signed, Sealed, Delivered," an easy favorite to get the crowd's attention and bring their energy up. It's one of the group's songs in which Jerome takes a leading role, using his own performance energy to set the tone for the Stevie Wonder classic. As far as Jerome remembers, the song was off to a great start, despite feeling a little out of it from his cold

RICE WITH GANDULES (PIGEON PEAS)

Side dish

SERVES 8

This popular Puerto Rican recipe is best served with pork. Pigeon peas can also be swapped out for pink beans.

PREP: 5 MINUTES **COOK: 25 MINUTES**

INGREDIENTS

1 tablespoon olive oil

⅓ cup sofrito

2 tablespoons tomato paste or ⅓ cup tomato sauce

16 ounces water

1 ½ teaspoons sazón

1 teaspoons adobo seasoning

15-ounce can gandules (pigeon peas), drained and rinsed

1 teaspoon garlic powder

2 cups rice

Heat olive oil in a 6-quart caldero or Dutch oven. Sauté the sofrito for 1 minute. Add the tomato paste or sauce, sazón, adobo, gandules, and garlic powder. Let simmer for 2–3 minutes.

Add rice and water. Sprinkle a dash of salt and a small drizzle of olive oil to reduce sticking. Bring to a boil. Cover and cook until rice has absorbed the liquids.

When rice is finished cooking, remove from heat, fluff with a fork, and serve.

SNC High Note: This can be made into a main entree by dicing pork and adding it to the recipe.

medications. Moments later, Jerome was flat on his back, with a view of all the guys standing over him, looking concerned. He realized he lost consciousness just after the opening line of the song. Jerome's inclination was to keep going and continue singing, but the guys insisted he get medical attention while they moved on to the next song.

Backstage, the medical team gave Jerome oxygen and lots of water. They cooled him down a bit, and then Jerome insisted on getting back out to the stage. He knows that in a cappella, every voice matters, and he made a commitment to the group and the audience to complete the performance. Jerome was back on stage a few songs later, and they finished the set exactly as planned. It was a relief to be able to finish the performance. Although he knows that health is critical, he also cares very deeply about showing up and not letting down people who rely on him.

In all of their time together, Straight No Chaser has had very few incidents in which illness has left the group short of a voice. Members rarely miss a performance, and when they do, the guys make every effort possible to adjust so the audience doesn't miss out on any aspect of the show. The guys rearrange songs, learn new vocal parts, and change set lists to emphasize the vocalists that are on stage. The group understands the importance of remaining healthy and well, and they trust one another to do what they need to do to bring their best selves to the stage. Sometimes this means limiting after-show drinks and socializing. Other times, it means actually taking really intentional rest days or planning time away from the group to rest and recuperate before the next tour or recording session. They are, after all, a brotherhood: each man is looking out for the others, and every man matters.

Straight No Chaser encourages the audience to record their performances and share photos with friends and family. After all, the group landed a record deal based on live concert footage. To this day, Jerome is surprised no video of his Wolf Trap fainting episode has surfaced. He likes to think it's because Chasers respect the dedication of the group and wouldn't want to put Jerome out. What he *really* believes is that, at that time, way back in 2012, fans were still wary of using their phones and devices to record performances. Since he fainted during the first at-bat during "Signed, Sealed, Delivered," fans didn't even have their phones out to record him dropping it like it's hot. And for that (and many other things), he's grateful.

Creating the Chasers

Kathie Lee Gifford is the original Chaser, at least in name and story. In 2008, less than a year after being signed to Atlantic Records, Straight No Chaser had their first professional appearances on national television. The first was the beloved *Christmas in Washington* special that ran on TNT for thirty-three consecutive years, and the second was a performance on NBC's *Today Show* with hosts Kathie Lee Gifford and Hoda Kotb. Backstage before the show, Kathie Lee asked the group what the correct term for their fans should be. Groupies? Followers? And then she took matters into her own hands and suggested one more option: Chasers? The moment they heard it, the guys all knew that Kathie Lee Gifford just coined the term for their rapidly growing fanbase. When the cameras flipped on, Jerome and Dan Ponce took up the roles as spokesmen for the group during the on-air interview with Kathie Lee and Hoda. The cameras were rolling, and when the question came up about their fans, Jerome quickly chimed in with her newly minted phrase "Chasers" loud and clear. Kathie Lee declared herself the group's oldest Chaser, settling the matter once and for all.

That first *Today Show* appearance marked an exceptional moment for the group. It was Straight No Chaser's first holiday season as a professional group. The day of their *Today* appearance, their first official album, *Holiday Spirits*, was out and quickly rising on the Billboard charts. *Holiday Spirits* remained the number one selling album for fourteen days on Amazon, and it reigned as the number one album on iTunes for five days. In early January 2009, the album hit its peak spot of 46 in the Billboard 200 chart—a major feat for the debut album of a new (not to mention a cappella) group.

The December 2008 appearance on *Today* was the first of many for the group. Over the years, Straight No Chaser has returned for live performances, holiday specials, and special occasions. One such occasion caught Jerome by surprise. In December 2015, Straight No Chaser was on yet another holiday tour. Jerome was antsy during this tour: his wife, Kristen, whom he met after she attended a Straight No Chaser show in Atlantic City, was due with their first child. In the early afternoon on December 5, Jerome got the call he had been anticipating. Kristen's water had broken, and it was time for Jerome to become a dad.

The group was mid-tour, with shows in Maryland and Pennsylvania that week. Jerome and Kristen lived in Florida, so the logistics were hurried. Jerome

SOUTHERN CARAMEL LAYERED CAKE

Dessert

SERVES 16

PREP: 15 MINUTES   **COOK: 2 HOURS**

CAKE

1 box mix of yellow cake

1 cup milk

⅓ cup butter or margarine, melted and cooled

1 teaspoon vanilla

3 eggs

CARAMEL ICING

3 cups granulated sugar, divided

1 stick unsalted butter

1 cup half-and-half, plus a little more

Dash of salt

2 tablespoons water

2 teaspoons vanilla

INSTRUCTIONS

Heat oven to 350°F for glass pans; 325°F for dark or nonstick pans.

Prepare two 9-inch cake pans by greasing and flouring.

In a large bowl, beat all cake ingredients with an electric mixer on low speed 1 minute, scraping bowl constantly, then on medium speed 2 minutes.

Divide batter between the prepared cake pans; bake and cool as directed on the box.

Prepare to make your icing; note that you will want to have all of your icing ingredients ready to go before you start cooking.

Using a large saucepan, pour 2 ½ cups sugar, butter, half-and-half, and salt, heat over medium until *almost* boiling. At the same time, in a small skillet, place ½ cup sugar with 2 tablespoons water and stir to combine; melt this sugar syrup until it becomes an amber color; you do not want to stir the syrup, but you should pick up the skillet and swirl/shake the mixture to ensure the sugar does not burn.

Once the sugar syrup is fully melted, pour the syrup into the first pan with the milk mixture. Cook on medium, stirring constantly until it reaches 235°F. Remove the saucepan from heat, pour mixture into a large bowl or

a stand mixer bowl, stir in vanilla, and let it cool for about 15 minutes.

Mix on medium speed or use a hand mixer on low-to-medium and whip until the caramel becomes frosting consistency, which can be up to 20 minutes.

Add icing between layers of cake, let the layers set, and then cover the rest of the cake with your icing.

SNC High Note: Jerome recommends being prepared to eat the whole cake. Not just one slice. The whole thing. Proceed with delicious caution.

Jerome triumphantly waving a "terrible towel" in the air with a sly grin during a performance in Pittsburgh. *Credit: Mitch Straub*

hung up the phone with Kristen and told the guys what was going on. Then, as all Straight No Chaser members do, his thoughts turned to the Chasers and the upcoming performance. It wasn't like Jerome to skip a show, but if there was ever a time to leave the guys, this was it. He didn't want to leave the audience with any questions or confusion about his absence. After all, by this time in Straight No Chaser's career, they had formed a contingent of loyal Chasers whom they loved and appreciated as friends. Jerome grabbed his phone, made a video for the audience to share the news about his growing family, and passed it off to the guys to share on the onstage screen while he was away.

He left for the airport right away and arrived in Florida around 6 p.m. that same evening after receiving his wife's call. Their daughter, Aaliyah, arrived healthy overnight. Jerome stayed with Kristen and Aaliyah that day and overnight, sharing updates with Chasers via his Twitter account. Somewhere along the way, news of Jerome and Kristen's new addition made its way to the *Today Show* team. The next morning, Jerome got a call from the show's producers congratulating him. They wanted to get him on camera, celebrating the arrival of his daughter. Jerome, as a novice dad, quickly agreed to the video interview. He ran in to share the news with Kristen, and just a day after giving birth, Jerome broadcast the new family on *Today*. It was a charming and sweet moment, but also one that makes Jerome and Kristen laugh today. "I realized that putting my wife and newborn on TV in a live national interview just a day after coming home with our first child is a bit of a new-dad moment I may never live down."

Sharing the news with *Today*, Chasers, and audiences around the world felt right to Jerome. It was the beginning of something new for him and his family, of course, but it was also a beautiful full-circle moment. The *Today Show* was where the "Chasers" name was solidified, and it was where Jerome got to announce the arrival of his family's next generation of Chasers. Straight No Chaser had brought Jerome the career he always wanted, made it possible for him to meet the love of his life, and announce his newest little love. Why not share his joy with the world?

VERSE 2

JASPER SMITH

Jasper Smith Is All Right

Winters in Indiana are messy on their worst days and utterly charming on their best days. There are holiday lights, Christmas decorations at all of the shops along Main Street, high school winter performances, and plenty of family reunions. This was the setting of one of Jasper's best memories: the day he got the call from Straight No Chaser to join the professional group.

Jasper had seen SNC perform at the Chicago Theatre several weeks earlier during their 2019 fall tour. He caught up with them after the show, glad to see the guys again. The SNC network never failed to surprise Jasper. He always felt like part of the SNC brotherhood despite being much younger than the members of the professional group. When DR texted Jasper a few days before Christmas, it didn't strike Jasper as odd or unexpected. However, the FaceTime call that followed was slightly out of the ordinary, and when nine faces appeared on screen, Jasper knew that something big was going on. Jasper's eyes were supposed to be on the road. He was on the way to the grocery store in his hometown to pick up a few items for his mom to prepare for the holidays. The guys on the other end realized quickly that Jasper was driving, and the first part of that evening's conversation was a series of "HANG UP!" shouts from his friends.

Jasper shares a laugh with the group just before the show starts. *Credit: Josh Adams*

Jasper smartly took their advice and safely got to the grocery store, where he called the group back—this time, parked and able to focus on whatever the group was going to tell him next.

"What are you doing on Sunday?"

Straight No Chaser invited Jasper to join them to watch a series of their shows in California starting just days after Christmas. DR was getting ready to leave the group, and they wanted Jasper to join. But first, they knew that he needed to see what life on the road was really like. Jasper was on the first flight out the next morning. The guys knew that Jasper could sing. But did his personality fit? After days on the road and several live performances, SNC decided that Jasper would be a great addition. They offered him an official spot in the group, and he was publicly introduced to their fan base in February 2020.

While he had known various members of Straight No Chaser for more than a decade, he had yet to work with the professional group. His transition into the group would include eventually learning hundreds of songs and their related choreography, as well as fitting in with eight other personalities. But 2020 presented an additional challenge. Without touring and meeting fans in person, their first introduction to Jasper would be through the many virtual performances titled *Quarantine Sessions*, which the group posted throughout the summer of 2020. It wasn't until a series of livestream concerts in December 2020 that Jasper was able to show more of his personality, and that he could both sing *and* dance.

Jasper finally got the chance to perform with the group onstage for the very first time nearly a year after he earned his spot in Straight No Chaser. The group decided to get together and livestream ten shows over the internet, directly to their supportive fan base. Jasper was ready but admittedly nervous. Despite his background as a performer and being part of musical groups in the past, this opportunity felt different to him. He wasn't sure if his fellow SNC members had any lingering doubts about his ability to perform on stage with the group, but if they did, he wanted to squash them for good. With ten shows and ten different set lists, Jasper was faced with a new kind of challenge: to learn the choreography and moves for all of the shows in a matter of days. He needed to memorize the moves to more than fifty songs, and he would need to do it primarily on his own. He watched YouTube to see Straight No Chaser's

Jasper crosses the stage during sound check. *Credit: Josh Adams*

previous dance moves and teach them to himself. This was showtime, and Jasper wasn't there to mess around. He rehearsed, practiced, and called on the guys for impromptu hallway dance sessions to make sure he knew what he was doing. He had worked with the music for more than a month, ensuring he got his parts exactly right. When it was time for the lights to go up and the show to start streaming, Jasper was as prepared as possible. He gave his performances his all and left nothing behind, singing and performing as best as he could to a completely empty venue. There was no clapping, no cheering, no celebration

HONEY LAVENDER GREYHOUND

Cocktail

COCKTAIL

2 ounces vodka

2 ounces grapefruit juice

2 tablespoons honey lavender simple syrup (see below)

Rosemary sprig, to garnish

SIMPLE SYRUP

½ cup water

½ cup honey

1 tablespoon dried lavender

Fill a rocks glass with ice and let chill.

Create your simple syrup by bringing water, honey, and lavender to a boil; reduce heat and simmer for 15 minutes. Remove from heat and let the mixture steep for 1 hour; then remove lavender by straining into a glass jar with lid.

Create your cocktail by pouring vodka, grapefruit juice, and syrup into chilled rocks glass. Stir, garnish, and enjoy.

as he completed his first performances with the group. Just the echoes of a completely vacant performance hall.

Despite plenty of congratulations from members of SNC, their manager, and their crew, Jasper was still curious about whether he had truly done what he set out to do. He got that confirmation from an unlikely source: Jerome's father, who has a history of marking a show's high points by shouting a loud, drawn out "Allllll riiiiiight" into the performance venue. After Jasper's first solo, Jerome's dad sent a message to Jerome to share with Jasper: a great, big "All right" from the man himself.

Jasper Smith is all right.

Negative Test, Positive Vibes

There's truly no way to prepare for being a professional musician during a pandemic. When the coronavirus took a hold of the American entertainment industry, Straight No Chaser was one of the thousands of musical groups that felt the impact. In early March 2020, the group had high hopes for the year ahead, and they gathered together for the first photoshoot and rehearsals that included Jasper. Multiple tours were on-sale, and the group was planning for a new album.

In just a matter of days after that weekend rehearsal, things started to take a turn. With the scope of the pandemic growing daily, the group first bumped concert dates from spring to the summer, and many were rescheduled for 2021. They had to find a way to stay connected to their fans in this unprecedented situation.

By the end of March, they had started sharing virtual performances, singing from the comfort of their homes. They hosted virtual happy hours, and released live footage from previous concerts, connecting with fans across the world. These virtual performances came to be known as the "Quarantine Sessions," complete with song requests from fans, and "Reclusive Exclusive" versions of songs they had not yet performed together. By early summer, it was clear to the group that their hope to still go out on their fall tour would be dashed. Live in-person events were canceled one after another. The group was challenged to come up with safe, online events to replace them.

The group decided to try something new: a series of virtual, live concerts from the stage at the MGM National Harbor Casino outside of Washington, DC. Fans got to watch from the comfort of their homes, but the guys were a bit outside of their comfort zone, without the feedback from a live audience. Virtual performances eliminate the space between performers and the Chasers: each Chaser was able to be in the front row at as many performances as they wanted.

In most ways, the performances were like a normal SNC show; the guys joked on stage, hit their notes, told stories between songs, and put all of their energy into creating a great experience for the audience. The one glaring difference was that they were singing to an empty room. There were no people smiling back at them, and no applause or cheering. High energy numbers simply . . . ended. Performing without audience interaction was hard, but they wanted to give their fans at home something to smile about. They were willing to do whatever it took to show them how much they appreciated their flexibility and loyalty to the group. In the end, Straight No Chaser was proud to bring their show into the homes of so many people who had supported them in-person for years and years. Straight No Chaser would simply not exist if it wasn't for the fans who have been steadfast in their support of the group, even being incredibly receptive to the changes and challenges of supporting the group in 2020.

Jasper and the Ukulele

Jasper Smith isn't the first Jasper to know how to win over an audience with musical charms. Growing up in Vincennes, Indiana, Jasper comes from a family of musicians and music lovers. Jasper's namesake, his suspender-wearing great-grandfather, was known for carrying around a ukulele—a fact that somehow makes sense if you know SNC's Jasper. There's something about a ukulele that makes sense about Jasper's story: a bit of youthfulness, charm, and a healthy dose of optimism. Jasper, who also plays the ukulele, has learned from his family the importance of music to gather people together and spark some fun.

GREAT-GRANDMA ERMA'S APPLE CRISP

Dessert

SERVES 6

A classic apple crisp dessert straight from the kitchen of Jasper's Great-Grandma Erma. You can't go wrong with Great-Grandma Erma!

PREP: 15 MINUTES   **COOK: 45 MINUTES**

INGREDIENTS

6 pink apples, peeled and chopped

2 tablespoons granulated sugar

1 ¾ teaspoon ground cinnamon (divided)

1 ½ teaspoon lemon juice

1 cup light brown sugar

¾ cup old fashioned oats

¾ cup all-purpose flour

½ cup cold unsalted butter, diced into small cubes

Pinch of salt

Butter an 8 × 8 baking dish or prep with non-stick cooking spray.

Add chopped apples, granulated sugar, ¾ teaspoon cinnamon, and lemon juice to a large mixing bowl and mix to coat apples well. Pour apple mixture into 8 × 8 baking dish.

In a separate mixing bowl, use a mixer to blend the brown sugar, oats, flour, diced butter, and salt until the mixture is combined yet crumbly. Spread the crumble over top of the apples.

Bake at 350° for 40–45 minutes, until bubbly and golden brown.

Remove from the oven, serve, and enjoy!

The 1996 movie *That Thing You Do!* made an impact on Jasper. The movie follows the story of a one-hit wonder pop group in the 1960s. After watching that movie, Jasper knew that he wanted to be a musician: a bass player. He recovered his mom's old acoustic guitar and started learning how to play. As a six-year-old, Jasper knew that he wanted to play whenever he could. His parents got him enrolled in guitar lessons with the local instructor, who ended up being the same mentor who recruited Jasper to join a rock band nearly a decade later. And so it went: Jasper started playing whenever possible, and he fit right into his family full of musicians.

Jasper could draw a circle on a map with a twenty-minute radius around his childhood home and capture nearly all of his relatives in Indiana. The Original Jasper, the one with the ukulele, wasn't the only family member who influenced him in his childhood. Jasper's father was one of six children, and Jasper and his younger brother, Lincoln, were two of nineteen cousins. Family get-togethers were chock full of snacks, laughter, and music. Music is strong in the Smith family. Jasper's mom enjoyed singing ("My mom has a really beautiful singing voice," he gushed), one uncle is a concert pianist, and another uncle was a theater performer on and off Broadway.

Despite this past, it was the Straight No Chaser viral video that changed Jasper's course in life. The "12 Days of Christmas" performance turned the a cappella world upside down when it hit the internet in 2006. Even the best gamblers in the world wouldn't have put money on the fact that a nearly decade-old video of ten guys, dressed in suits, standing in a line on the Musical Arts Center stage at Indiana University would have a direct and hard-hitting impact on Jasper's future, but they would be wrong.

In his senior year, Jasper made some choices. He had committed to Butler University in Indianapolis. He had received a scholarship to attend for swimming. His housing deposit had already been turned in. The check was cashed. And then the stars aligned, one by one. In February of Jasper's senior year, Butler University disbanded its men's swimming program for financial reasons. Suddenly, Jasper's commitment to the school was

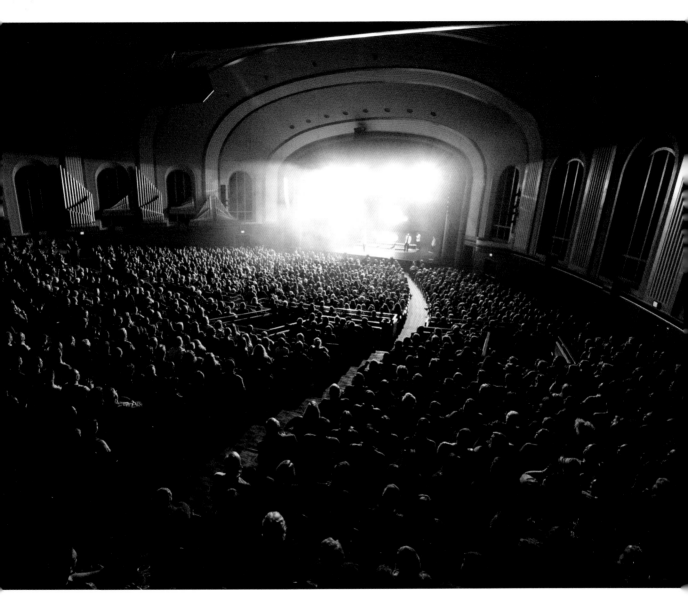

The lights shining across the audience at a Straight No Chaser show at the IU Auditorium in Bloomington, Indiana. *Credit: Evan De Stefano Photography*

ITALIAN BEEF

Main Course

SERVES 12

Italian beef offers a warm comfort food that's perfect for a Chicago winter day.

PREP: 15 MINUTES   COOK: 5–6 HOURS

INGREDIENTS

2 tablespoons olive oil

1 teaspoon minced garlic

4 lb. chuck or rump roast

2 cups beef broth

16 ounce jar sliced pepperoncini peppers with juice

1 sliced onion

1 packet Italian dressing mix

Brown your roast by heating olive oil and garlic in skillet or Dutch oven; sear each side before placing the roast in the slow cooker. Add roast to the crock pot. Pour in beef broth to the crock pot. Add in peppers with their juices. Place sliced onion on top of roast. Empty packet of Italian dressing on top of onions and roast.

Cook in slow cooker for 5–6 hours on high or 8–9 hours on low until beef easily shreds.

Remove the beef and shred it fully.

Return the shredded beef to the slow cooker and let sit for 15–20 minutes before serving.

Serve on hoagie buns; top with additional sliced peppers and add provolone cheese if desired.

SNC High Note: Use the juice! Spoon that on your sandwich. Don't be afraid to use your bread as a sponge.

Jasper works on his choreography during a rehearsal alongside Steve and Tyler.
Credit: Josh Adams

severed. It was still a great university option in Indianapolis, and there was no major reason to change his course. That was true until Straight No Chaser did a cannonball right into Jasper's life when his mom showed him the video of "The 12 Days of Christmas." Jasper had never seen a group quite like Straight No Chaser, and something about the performance clicked for him. The guys were funny, they had personality, they performed as a group, and yet each personality had a place. It was different from what Jasper knew about a cappella, which until then had been barbershop quartets and mimics of *The Music Man*.

Making it to Straight No Chaser was not a simple path. In fact, Jasper got rejected from the group, twice, but it never deterred him. In fact, rejection became part of Jasper's story in the strongest way. He tried out for the collegiate group again, and the third time was the charm. He spent three years as a collegiate member of IU's Straight No Chaser. After graduating, he stayed the course by performing with Dan Ponce's spinoff a cappella group, Gentleman's Rule, for two years in Chicago. Feeling a financial pinch and the need for health insurance, Jasper got a stable yet cringeworthy job of selling copiers. He kept his musician life alive through weekend and evening musical gigs, and even a two-year stint with a wedding band. Rejection wove back into Jasper's story when he tried out for the group when Don Nottingham left the group in 2017, but he didn't make the cut. True to his commitment, Jasper didn't let it deter him. He stayed ready, stayed committed to music, and he trusted that things would work out when the time was right. And when he received that call from Straight No Chaser in December 2019, Jasper knew it was the right time for him.

The SNC Chaplain

One important yet unofficial role in Straight No Chaser has nothing to do with music. The SNC Chaplain started with Ryan Ahlwardt, who gathered the group together in prayer before shows as a way to calm nerves,

WHITE CHICKEN CHILI

Main Course

SERVES 7

This white chicken chili is excellent for gatherings. It tastes even better with SNC playing in the background. Chef's promise.

PREP: 10 MINUTES   **COOK: 40 MINUTES**

INGREDIENTS

1 tablespoon salad oil

1 lb. boneless chicken, chopped into bite size pieces

1 chopped onion

1 clove garlic

1 teaspoon cumin

2 15-ounce cans white beans

1 15-ounce can garbanzo beans/chickpeas

1 15-ounce can white corn

¼ lb. Monterey Jack cheese

1 4.5-ounce can green chilies

2–3 jalapeno peppers

Salt and pepper to taste

Sauté chicken, onion, garlic, and cumin in large saucepan with oil until chicken is no longer pink, onion is soft, and spices are fragrant.

Add beans, corn, cheese, chilies, and sliced jalapeno peppers to the saucepan.

Cook on low for 2 hours to combine flavors, stirring occasionally.

SNC High Note: Add 1 cup of chicken broth to make the chili more like a soup. Again, served best with SNC playing in the background. We cannot emphasize this enough.

re-center themselves, and have a moment of quiet. The routine was quickly accepted as part of the group's pre-show ritual, and the tradition has lived on ever since.

The SNC Chaplain is, of course, not an actual chaplain, and none of the guys would claim it as such. Instead, the SNC Chaplain serves the group by uniting the members together in quiet reflection, often accompanied by a Bible verse, a prayer, and a quick moment to set intentions for the performance ahead. When Ryan Ahlwardt left the group, DR gladly accepted the role. When Jasper first joined the group, he traveled to California to watch them perform together and get a sense of what life on the road would be like as a professional member of SNC. One of the memories he carried with him from that trip was watching the guys huddle together before a show, united in prayer. It stuck with him, and he felt immediately comforted by the presence of faith in the group. No one had asked him about his own beliefs or religion prior to joining SNC, but when Jasper witnessed the group coming together, he knew that this was another aspect of the group that made him feel so at home among them.

There's no loud religion in Straight No Chaser. There's no requirement for believing any one thing in particular. There's no system or demagogue or commitment that unites the guys to any specific faith or church or denomination. It's quieter than that, and significantly more subtle. Jasper, who has no reservations about declaring that he is a man of faith, loved the quiet reverence that was part of the group. He has no idea whether the other members of Straight No Chaser have strong faiths or involvement with religious groups. Jasper knows that it doesn't really matter. When he saw that the men came together for a quick moment of reflection, it signaled something greater than what a Bible verse or prayer could communicate: a commitment to serving a larger purpose. This aspect of Straight No Chaser reinforced for Jasper what he already knew and loved about the group: they were willing to show up as individuals with a passion and create amazing music as a group, and they worked with the understanding that their sound is only possible when they look at the whole picture and never one guy alone. It's that mission of knowing that ego won't survive and the whole is better than any individual part that makes Jasper happy to serve as SNC Chaplain.

Jasper was tapped for the role by DR as he was preparing to leave the group. In the years since the college group, DR and Jasper had gotten to know each other and became good friends. Through their friendship, they discussed important life values, and Jasper shared his perspectives on faith. DR thought that Jasper would be the right person to step up and take over as SNC Chaplain, and his thoughts were confirmed. After one of DR's final performances, he clapped Jasper on the back and nominated him as the next SNC Chaplain. Jasper simply said, "I can do that."

The thing about a cappella is that it's inherently synergistic: it would never work if each of the guys thought his own role was more or less important than anyone else's. A cappella only works if there's a larger purpose that everyone shares. In his role as SNC Chaplain, Jasper is channeling that vision of a larger purpose. He has everything he needs to do the small components of a big job, including a Bible app to keep his favorite passages at the ready and a lifelong history of prayers to call upon. More than that, Jasper knows and understands that even a quick, two-minute huddle backstage can be a powerful way to remind himself and the others to appreciate the opportunity they have to pursue their dreams together, on stage, as Straight No Chaser.

For Jasper, there was no better way to be welcomed to the group than being designated as the unofficial SNC Chaplain.

The guys get a tour of the facilities at the Indianapolis 500 from J. Douglas Boles, President of the Indianapolis Motor Speedway, before singing "Back Home Again in Indiana" at the race in 2015. *Credit: David Britz*

TYLER TREPP

New Track Tradition

"New Track Tradition" is the headline of the newspaper article that Tyler Trepp has hanging in his home. The *Indianapolis Star* chronicled the moment that Straight No Chaser stepped in at the 2015 Indianapolis 500 to sing "Back Home Again in Indiana." Signed by every member who was at the performance, the framed piece is a marker of a milestone moment for the group and a personal reminder for Tyler to appreciate the opportunities that come from being a part of the group.

Growing up, Tyler watched the Indy 500 with his family. He lived in Iowa, and each year, his family would travel to their lake house to celebrate Memorial Day weekend. Like clockwork, his family would tune into the Indy 500 on Sunday. For Tyler, it wasn't so much that he was a die-hard racing fan. In fact, he's still not a die-hard racing fan. But people across the world tune into the Indy 500 because it's a tradition, and it never fails to make Tyler proud to have been a part of that tradition in a big way, even for just one day.

On May 24, 2015, Straight No Chaser's voices reverberated through the Indianapolis Motor Speedway. The sound reverberated around the two and a half mile track, as the group sang "Back Home Again in Indiana." It was the first time since 1972 that the fans would sing along to a voice other than that of Jim Nabors, who had performed the traditional song every year until his 2014 retirement.

PORK TENDERLOIN SANDWICH

Main Course

SERVES 4

Breaded pork tenderloin sandwiches are an Indiana classic dish and known to be a main food at the Indianapolis 500 event.

PREP: 20 MINUTES   **COOK: 20 MINUTES**

INGREDIENTS

4 pork tenderloins, about 4 ounces each, sliced against the grain to open like a book

1 egg

2 tablespoons milk

¼ teaspoon garlic powder

¼ teaspoon onion powder

¼ teaspoon Lawry's seasoned salt

¼ teaspoon dried oregano

1 teaspoon salt

¼ teaspoon black pepper

1 ½ cups bread crumbs

½ cup oil for frying

4 rolls

INSTRUCTIONS

Tenderize pork cutlets until they are about ¼ inch thick.

In a bowl, beat egg and add milk; whisk in garlic powder, onion powder, seasoned salt, oregano, salt, and pepper until well combined.

In a separate bowl, measure out bread crumbs.

Prepare a plate with parchment paper or wax paper to place pork loin onto once breaded.

Dip each pork cutlet into egg mixture, then into bread crumbs. Be sure to coat thoroughly. Once covered on all sides, place the pork on the prepared plate. Do not stack.

In a frying pan, heat oil until shimmering and ready to fry. Fry each cutlet, one at a time, in the pan, flipping once each side is golden brown (about 6–8 minutes).

Place on paper towels to absorb oil.

Repeat until all cutlets are fried.

Serve on toasted rolls with optional toppings of your choice: ketchup, mustard, mayonnaise, pickle, tomato, lettuce, and/or onion.

SNC High Note: The perfection of this sandwich is that it's an imperfect sandwich. Let your pork tenderloin hang over the roll by an inch on each side for the true Hoosier effect!

Straight No Chaser was there to see Nabors's final performance. The Indy 500 production team had been in touch with the group in anticipation of Nabors's retirement, and they coordinated for all ten members to attend the 2014 events to get a taste of the excitement of performing at the Indy 500 and the fanfare that came along with it. They marked their presence on the red carpet with an impromptu performance and got to mingle with the celebrity guests at the famed Pagoda, the ten-level, glass-enclosed building that overlooks the 2.605-mile racetrack, while they watched the Indy 500 race. They performed that night at the Snakepit Ball, now called the 500 Festival Off the Grid, at the upscale Indiana Roof Ballroom. In December 2014, at one of their performances at the Murat Theater in Indianapolis, the group announced their upcoming Indy 500 performance, with local television stations there to capture the news.

In May 2015, Straight No Chaser returned in Indianapolis for the big race weekend. As Tyler recalls, part of the appeal to the Indy 500 production team of having Straight No Chaser perform at the famed event was their deep roots in the people and traditions of Indiana. Tyler knew that the group was stepping into a legend's shoes by taking over for Jim Nabors after his final performance the year before. He had witnessed the fans' admiration for the event, the song, and the race festivities. This performance of "Back Home Again in Indiana" was about honoring what the Indy 500 and all of its fans expected: a song that brings the people of Indiana together.

Inhaling the classic racetrack smells of hot asphalt, tire rubber, and gasoline, Straight No Chaser took to the main performance stage. They dressed in coordinating short sleeve, collared shirts, black pants, and white-soled sneakers. Adding a few opening notes and melodies to start off the song, the group performed to their largest live crowd ever; a quarter of a million people packed the stands and the infield. To Tyler, it was like singing a hymn in church. People participated by singing along, all of them there to experience this moment in time together, feeling the pull of the community and the values of what the Indy 500 stood for in this community of people.

That performance, and the events that surrounded it, was a memory-jar moment for Tyler, who still smiles when talking about the experience. Even the opportunity to have his spotlight moment dimmed by the Indianapolis Colts quarterback Andrew Luck, who walked behind them on the red carpet, obviously pulling attention from the group, was a great experience. How often does an NFL quarterback follow you down a red carpet, after all?

Cruising Into Music

Tyler grew up in Urbandale, Iowa, doing all of the things that kids in Urbandale, Iowa, grow up doing. He played soccer and basketball, sang in the church choir, joined the band in middle school, and expanded his interests in high school by adding show choir, jazz band, and nights out to hear the latest concerts in nearby downtown Des Moines. He loved the trumpet, though he learned later that his trumpet skills didn't quite compete with Seggie's talents, a fact that he freely and consistently admits. While he was in high school, Tyler leveraged his singing skills and penchant for performance through his own a cappella group, "The Sophtones," that he formed with three other members of the choir. A fellow show choir member gave Tyler an album of a group of singers he had never heard of: Straight No Chaser. Tyler's parents would confirm that once Tyler sets his mind on something, it's hard to dissuade him. After hearing Straight No Chaser, Tyler wanted to be a part of it, and he wasn't going to wait until college to give it a try.

On a weekend trip to Bloomington to visit the campus, Tyler had his first in-person interaction with the collegiate Straight No Chaser group through the form of Jermaine Miles. That day, Jermaine let Tyler shadow him for the day along with Tyler's friend Adam Rich, another member of Tyler's high school a cappella group who later became a two-year member of IU's Straight No Chaser. Jermaine told them that the collegiate group opened auditions to seniors in high school, and if they were serious about a cappella and being a part of the group, they could come back in the spring to audition. In March, Tyler and Adam returned to the Bloomington campus, auditioned, and both were invited to join the group that fall. That sealed the deal for Tyler. He was eager to do something different than his peers, most of whom attended in-state schools. Tyler had already received a scholarship to attend the University of Nebraska to play the trumpet, but the allure of Straight No Chaser dominated his thoughts. That fall, Tyler enrolled at IU as a freshman, and one of the newest members of IU's Straight No Chaser.

Tyler was a telecommunications major on paper, but in reality, he feels like he majored in Straight No Chaser because of all the time he put into evening rehearsals, weekend performances, and hanging out with other members. As a non–music major, Tyler didn't have to perform recitals or pass vocal skills tests during his time there, but Tyler recognized that Indiana University produces incredible vocalists, and he took advantage by enrolling in several music classes. He tapped into professors, graduate students, music majors, and his Straight No Chaser peers to help him develop his singing abilities.

His telecommunications classes also confirmed a few things for Tyler, which was that his passion was really in music and not in telecommunications, and that he definitely, absolutely preferred to be in front of the camera and not on the technical side behind the equipment. He would always volunteer to be the onscreen news anchor in any simulation productions that his classmates were putting together. That served him well during his time with the collegiate Straight No Chaser, and soon after when he was a part of an at-sea a cappella group on a cruise ship.

As it turned out, Tyler never had to tap into his telecommunications degree at all. After graduating from IU in 2007, Tyler connected with Mike Landau, a previous member of the collegiate Straight No Chaser group, who was working with four-part a cappella groups for cruise lines and needed a new crew for upcoming tours on other ships. Mike tapped Tyler to create a new four-man group, and Tyler knew just the people. He had been musical director for Straight No Chaser during three of his four years in the college group, so he knew what he was looking for when it came to a mix of vocals, talent, and personality. Tyler formed Ocean's Four, a four-part a cappella group that included two collegiate Straight No Chaser alumni, and they set out to sea just months later in December 2007.

Singing for a living while on a cruise ship is a rare job that brings unique privileges. Tyler traveled across the world, got paid to sing every night, and was something of a mini celebrity in the microcosm of the cruise ship world. The group sang on the stages of massive cruise ships for up to fourteen days at a time; spending the day at the beach or relaxing on the ship, and singing at night. The ship docked for days at a time, and Tyler and the other quartet members could explore the world before getting back to sea. It was as dreamy as it gets

Tyler cutting a rug on stage. He admits it's a dream that he gets paid to travel and sing for people all over the world. *Credit: Evan De Stefano Photography*

when it comes to first jobs: Tyler still can't believe he got paid to sing and travel to places like Aruba, Cozumel, Playa del Carmen, Barbados, and Santorini (Tyler says, "I mean, I was putting money into my bank account doing these things. That's ridiculous!").

Cruising around the world felt like a dream, and Tyler knew that one day, he'd have to consider a life after the cruise ship gig was up. He thought maybe he'd go into advertising after his second six-month contract expired. Advertising had the right combination of entry-level jobs, easy relocation, and, at first glance,

"CHOOSE YOUR OWN ADVENTURE" RISOTTO

Main Course

SERVES 6–8

Inspired by a Betty Crocker recipe from long ago, this updated risotto recipe can be adjusted and altered with various spices to suit your taste. Channel Tyler's postcollege adventures as you build your own perfect variation of this dish.

PREP: 10 MINUTES   **COOK: 45 MINUTES**

INGREDIENTS

2 tablespoons extra virgin olive oil

1 onion, diced

2–3 garlic cloves, diced

1 teaspoon black pepper

1 ½ teaspoon coarse sea salt

2 cups rice (short grain is preferred)

4 cups chicken broth

1 teaspoon ground turmeric

1 15-ounce can garbanzo beans, drained

2 handfuls fresh spinach

½ cup grated Parmigiano-Reggiano

INSTRUCTIONS

Heat the oil in a large skillet.

Sauté onion for 10 minutes until it becomes translucent, then add garlic and sauté another 3–5 minutes; add salt and pepper.

Add rice to the onion and garlic; sauté for 1 minute, stirring the rice toast lightly.

Add broth and turmeric; cover and bring to a boil, then reduce to low; cook for roughly 35 minutes.

At 30 minutes, start checking your rice; you want it to be slightly runny—risotto should "fall" slightly when plated.

Stir in cheese; this will help the dish solidify slightly.

As soon as cheese is incorporated, remove from the heat and add spinach; stir until it wilts, then add the drained beans.

Check the flavor of your dish and adjust seasoning as necessary. Bon appétit!

SNC High Note: As you build your own risotto recipe, experiment with swapping out broths as you swap out the seasonings. It's a great way to subtly shift the flavors and enhance your spice selections.

lots of women in the career. That was the plan that never came to be as he set sail with his second contract in October 2008. In early 2009, Tyler tapped into the cruise ship's spotty and unreliable internet connection to check his email. Sitting in his small cabin aboard a massive cruise ship in the middle of the ocean, Tyler learned that two members of Straight No Chaser were moving on, and he was welcome to come audition for the group. The logistics of getting from the middle of the ocean to auditions in Chicago were challenging but Tyler set his mind to making it to Chicago in April. He called his booking agent, who agreed to let Tyler sit out an entire week of shows if he could find a replacement quartet to fill in.

"My agent called and told me I was a freaking lucky guy," Tyler said. Tyler found a replacement quartet and made it to Chicago. After the audition, he returned to the cruise ship life. He was back at sea bobbing up and down in the Caribbean when he got the news: Tyler Trepp was back with Straight No Chaser, now at a professional level.

Start Big, Funny in the Middle, End Big

Three of the four years that Tyler was part of the collegiate group, he was the musical director, charged with arranging the music, making sure every vocalist knows his part, and ensuring the combination of songs worked well together for shows. He used his college experience forming his at-sea group, Ocean's Four, and again when it came to creating medley arrangements for Straight No Chaser. Today, Tyler still works as one of the arrangers in SNC, primarily arranging cover songs, which means songs need to be deconstructed, arranged into sheet music, assigned to a specific vocalist, and rehearsed as a group. Every song requires different energy and different adjustments. Tyler doesn't strictly work on medleys, but he's quick to note that the medleys are some of the most fun arrangements that Straight No Chaser takes on.

Luckily, Tyler doesn't work alone, and his time in the collegiate SNC overlapped with Seggie Isho's. Their years together as collegiate performers were a great head start on their partnership in the professional group. Tyler and

Randy, Tyler, Seggie, and Mike rehearsing before a show at the IU Auditorium.
Credit: Evan De Stefano Photography

Seggie have used their strengths to create "The Movie Medley," "The Broadway Medley," and "The Disney Medley."

Straight No Chaser released "The Movie Medley" in 2015, but the brainstorming began long before the release. The idea was to take some of the most recognizable film scores, add humorous lyrics, and blend them together in an onstage performance that audiences would love.

Star Wars is undoubtedly one of the most recognizable film scores and was a must-include. Tyler's job was to arrange the music, and he leaned on Seggie to

TYLER'S CHICKEN WING DIP

Appetizer

SERVES 10

PREP: 5 MINUTES   COOK: 40 MINUTES

INGREDIENTS

8 ounces cream cheese, softened

1 cup Frank's RedHot®

2 cups shredded cheese

½ cup of bottled Ranch dressing

3 large chicken breasts, boiled and shredded

Grease the sides of a shallow baking dish (a pie pan or quiche pan will work).

Mix all ingredients in a large mixing bowl.

Spoon mixture into prepared baking dish.

Bake at 350°F for 35 minutes or until cheese is fully melted and mixture is bubbling.

SNC High Note: Serve with Fritos Scoops chips. You can offer carrot sticks and celery, too, but they usually serve as decoration.

Tyler singing during a performance. Even after years of touring, Tyler still loves to be onstage with Straight No Chaser. *Credit: Mitch Straub*

help put the words together. Without having seen all of the Star Wars movies, Seggie asked Tyler for a quick overview of the film series so he could get a sense of the story line they were working with.

"Well, at one point, he kisses his sister," Tyler explained.

That small nugget in the vast complexity of the Star Wars franchise became one of the key points of "The Movie Medley" because it brought the humor. Tyler follows a proven pattern for each of the major medleys: start big, go funny in the middle, and end big. Every medley component follows that pattern, and when

FRENCH 75

Cocktail

A classic gin and champagne drink that we raise in remembrance of the days we couldn't travel. Cheers to all of our worldwide tours, past, present, and future!

COCKTAIL

1.5 ounces gin

¾ ounce fresh lemon juice

¾ ounce simple syrup

2 or 3 ounces chilled champagne

SIMPLE SYRUP

¼ cup sugar

¼ cup water

Make simple syrup by combining water and sugar in a saucepan over medium heat. Whisk together until sugar is dissolved; remove from heat and cool completely.

Pour gin, lemon juice, and simple syrup in a cocktail shaker filled with ice. Shake vigorously and pour contents into champagne flute. Top with champagne and garnish with lemon peel if desired.

Serve and enjoy!

SNC High Note: Let's work smarter, not harder. You can make large batches of simple syrup and store them for up to six months in an airtight container in the refrigerator.

a character like Luke Skywalker kisses his sister, it's guaranteed to meet the criteria for funny in the middle.

The goal, according to Tyler, is always to make it entertaining. The bigger the laugh from the audience, the better, but the humor will fail if the music isn't just as strong. Tyler spends a lot of time considering how to smoothly transition from one song into the next.

Once a medley is together on paper, the members each have the chance to tweak it, put a personal touch to it, and adjust as they practice and perform the full medley. Says Tyler, "Things will change from the time we put it down as a demo to when we perform it. Sometimes, things seem a lot funnier to us than our audience thinks it is."

Luckily, the guys know when something lands, and they know when it just needs a minor adjustment to make the impact they want. With over eleven years of experience under his belt helping to arrange music for Straight No Chaser, Tyler knows one thing for sure: they started big with a viral hit, they're adding humor in the middle, and they will undoubtedly end big, too.

The Life and Times of (Collegiate) Straight No Chaser

In Tyler's sophomore year, the college group competed in the International Championship of Collegiate A Cappella, or ICCA. There were three rounds of competition, and Straight No Chaser knew there had to be something special about this performance. Inspired by another group's five-minute rendition of *The Wizard of Oz*, Straight No Chaser got to work creating a unique performance. The result was one of Tyler's favorite Straight No Chaser songs, and it remains a favorite today: "The Life and Times of Straight No Chaser."

"The Life and Times of Straight No Chaser" is a medley that covered the time from when the members were born to present day. They filled every second they could on the stage until they hit the competition limit of eleven minutes per group. Each member arranged part of it, singing and talking through their own story. "The Life and Times of Straight No Chaser" won them sectionals, regionals, and a ticket to New York City to perform for the national competition.

While they didn't place in the national competition, that performance won them a standing ovation—the only group to receive one that day.

That competition in 2005 earmarked one chapter in the life and times of Straight No Chaser. Other years that will stand out to Tyler in the life and times of the group include 2008, the year the group started their professional career, and for Tyler, 2009, the year he left his life at sea and joined the professional Straight No Chaser. And 2020 turned into another major chapter, when much of the group's business as usual came to a screeching halt as the world responded to the coronavirus and COVID-19.

Tyler, his wife Lauryn, and their two-year-old daughter, Carly, had to adjust to a new version of the life and times of Straight No Chaser. Concerts were canceled, tours delayed, and all of the in-person gatherings that normally fuel the group's momentum were gone. Tyler swapped in extra daddy duty: learning about ponytails, heading to toddler swim class, and getting his singing rejected by Carly, who prefers to sing lullabies and her favorite songs on her own.

The members of Straight No Chaser had to learn to be more flexible than ever before, even if it made the process of creating new music more challenging for the group. Instead of rehearsing and recording in person, each member used their own recording equipment at home to record their vocals. This process takes much longer than recording in person. If a note is off or a certain melody isn't working, it's often days before the arranger of that particular song will know. Every member has to submit their recorded part, which the song's arranger compiles together as one piece. If any part is off, that vocalist will re-record their piece, and then the song is put back together for the final arrangement.

The effort was worth it. The group regularly released videos on their YouTube channel and even managed to record an entire new Christmas album, which was released in in November 2020. For Tyler, in between parenting and remaining safe at home, it felt good to focus his energy on what he could do within the group in the time they couldn't be together on tour.

Whether it's adjusting a song to better land a joke, creating an eleven-minute medley to fit a competition, or turning to live-stream concerts and online performances during a global pandemic, it's all a day in the life and times of Straight No Chaser.

Charlie delivers one of his humorous introductions to an audience in Champaign, Illinois, in October 2019. *Credit: Evan De Stefano Photography*

VERSE 4

CHARLIE MECHLING

The Tiniest Fraternity in Chicago

Charlie Mechling remembers the summers he spent in Chicago with Straight No Chaser as a lot of hustle, a tiny bit of money, and a lot of laughter. For two summers, Charlie, Randy, Walter, Steve, Dan, Mike (Itkoff), DR, and Jerome called Chicago home. The guys were trying to build Straight No Chaser's reputation and make some money by taking on gigs as often as they could. They worked day jobs to pay rent and spent evenings and weekends making rounds across the Windy City. The equation isn't that hard to figure out. Five guys packed into a tiny apartment plus Chicago plus a little bit of money equals some of the best summers of Charlie's life.

In the moment, Charlie and the other Straight No Chaser guys loved the cramped lifestyle. They would come home after their day shifts and hang together, dreaming up their next move for Straight No Chaser. Building a music group from the ground up like they did isn't glamorous work. It takes a lot of long days, late nights, a tolerance of rejection, and an openness to any opportunity to get in front of people. Part of their pact for the summers was to take on as much work as they could manage, and there weren't many opportunities that they let pass by. Some of the gigs were amazing. The group sang the national anthem for the Chicago Cubs and Chicago White Sox, along with a plethora of summer festivals and private parties with some help courtesy

METROPOLITAN

Cocktail

Living the big city life is fun.

INGREDIENTS

2 ounces of vodka

2 ounces of Cointreau or Triple Sec

1 ounce fresh lime juice

1 ounce cranberry juice

Fill a cocktail shaker with ice.

Pour in all ingredients into a cocktail shaker and shake well.

Strain into a chilled stemmed glass.

***SNC High Note*: You can swap orange juice for the cranberry if you're in a pinch! Garnish with orange zest if you're feeling fancy.**

of connections via Randy's dad. The performance venues rarely caught the guys by surprise. The overlap of very bizarre settings and people who want to book an a cappella performance is low, but there is one that stands out in Charlie's memory: the casino boats.

There's an area outside Chicago in Hammond, Indiana, that is home to several casino riverboats. There were buildings constructed that served as gatekeepers to the boats. Guests would park their cars in the lot, walk through a small building, and then board the ships. All guests would filter through this entrance on their way to the main ship, and Straight No Chaser was there to greet them. But unlike other welcoming performances the group had performed, this one was particularly notable because of the small contraption that served as the stage. It was circular, and all ten guys would stand in the center of the circle to perform their fifteen-minute routine. The performance would conclude, and the circular stage would slowly take the guys, still on board, down to a lower level and out of sight of the guests walking by. They would wait twenty minutes, and the stage would bring them back up again. Over and over, Straight No Chaser was lifted and lowered from the main walkway to perform the same fifteen-minute routine for the entire night, going largely ignored by the guests on their way to the riverboats.

They thought it was amazing.

Steve, who wasn't twenty-one at the time, had to sneak onto the riverboats after the gig was up. They would drink $1 beers and gamble, squandering all the money they had just earned and still rolling on the high of being paid to do something they all loved to do. Being on any stage was enough to the guys, and there's a truth to that even today. Their summers in Chicago on that stage weren't unlike their experience growing Straight No Chaser. At the top, it was exciting to be on a strange, circular platform singing their hearts out. And, just like that, they would go underground again, working together as friends and improving their performance until it was time to take to the stage again.

Nights like those on the riverboats fueled their time in Chicago. To Charlie, those summers in Chicago were the real work of getting Straight No Chaser off the ground. There was the hustle and grind of working multiple jobs and doing performances in the evenings and on weekends. But there was also the more

CHARLIE MECHLING

relaxed side of life. They watched Cubs games, swapped work stories, and found local bars and neighborhood dives. They would plan cookouts with friends, and then move the grill inside and crack a window if it rained. It was life as a bunch of twenty-something guys living together in a big city as much as it was a group of aspiring, talented singers with their eyes on the future.

The East Coast Gig and the Donut Sign Debacle (Part One)

Charlie Mechling has been a part of Straight No Chaser since the group first formed. He has thousands of hours of memories and experiences with the group. He could pull from collegiate performances or professional tours around the world. He could name more than one wedding of other Straight No Chaser members that he's been in. There are countless dinners, nights out together, meetings, rehearsals, and phone calls. But, after twenty-five years together, there is—and will always be—only one donut sign incident.

Each of the guys who were part of Straight No Chaser at the time of the donut sign incident might give a different version of a similar story. In Charlie's mind, it went like this:

It was the spring of 1998. Straight No Chaser was still trying to gather momentum as a college group. It was tough to build a network in Indiana outside of IU, as there weren't many a cappella groups in the region. Most a cappella, at that time, had deeper roots on the East Coast, and that was where most competitions and larger performances happened. The group decided that instead of taking a typical college spring break, they would plan their own SNC spring break and create a tour along the East Coast. The plan was to book several shows during the week, drive from show to show, and crash on the couches of friends, family, and their a cappella connections along the way. The guys called around looking for opportunities to perform at colleges and universities that had an a cappella presence on campus. They forgot to consider the fact that if Indiana University was on spring break, there was a good chance that other schools would *also* be on spring break. Straight No Chaser booked just one actual gig for

Charlie enjoys a break from tour rehearsals and watches a win in Assembly Hall for the Hoosiers, on March 4, 2020. *Credit: Evan De Stefano Photography*

their entire East Coast tour: a show, in a classroom, at Boston College, which was as exciting as it reads, and needs no further attention. The guys also had two planned educational performances, one at Walter Chase's former high school in Bethlehem, Pennsylvania, and one at Patrick Hachey's former high school in Basking Ridge, New Jersey.

One gig was better than none, so Jerome, Patrick, Dan, Walt, DR, Steve, Randy, and Charlie packed their duffle bags and crammed into two cars. Half

HOMEMADE GLAZED DONUTS

Dessert or Main Course

SERVES 12

We don't judge your decision to eat donuts for your main meal, a quick snack in the afternoon, a sweet dessert in the evening, or some combination of all three.

PREP: 5 MINUTES   **COOK: 3 HOURS**

DONUTS

1 ¼ cups milk

2 ¼ teaspoons active dry yeast (one package)

2 eggs

1 stick butter, melted and cooled

¼ cup of granulated sugar

1 teaspoon salt

4 ¼ cups all-purpose flour; 1–2 handfuls for rolling out dough

2 quarts oil for frying

GLAZE

¼ cup whole milk

1 teaspoon vanilla extract

2 cups confectioners' sugar

INSTRUCTIONS

In a saucepan, heat milk over medium heat until it is about 90°F, then add yeast; mix lightly and let sit for 5 minutes.

Using a mixer (ideally a standing mixer with a dough hook), make the dough. Pour in the milk mixture, beat in the eggs, butter, sugar, and salt. Add half of the flour, mix until combined.

Slowly add the rest of the flour until the dough begins to pull away from the bowl. Remove the bowl from the stand, cover, and let rise at room temperature until it doubles in size, which is about an hour.

Flour a rolling pin and counter area to roll out dough to ½-inch thickness. Cut the donuts with a donut cutter or cookie cutters. Keep the donut centers to make donut holes.

Place cut donuts on two floured baking sheets, cover, and let rise for 45 minutes. Donuts will appear slightly puffy.

While your donuts rise, prepare your glaze by combining milk and vanilla in a small saucepan over medium heat; add the confectioners' sugar and whisk slowly until well combined; remove from heat, but keep glaze liquid by placing it on top of a bowl of hot water.

Prepare a cooling rack for the donuts by placing a rack on top of a baking sheet. Line with paper towels to absorb excess oil.

When your donut timer has 15 minutes left, heat oil to 375°F. Use a metal spatula or your hands to carefully add 2–3 donuts to the oil. Watch the donuts, as each side only needs 45–60 seconds to become golden and need to be flipped.

Flip your donuts using a slotted spoon, then promptly remove when both sides are golden.

Let excess oil drip off the donut, then dip in glaze. Let sit for 3–5 minutes before serving.

Charlie reviews sheet music on his iPhone during sound check in Champaign, Illinois.
Credit: Evan De Stefano Photography

of the crew jumped in Steve's car, and the other half piled into Randy's father's Chevy Suburban that Randy borrowed for the week. The first part of the trip went as planned. Straight No Chaser performed at Boston College in a lecture hall and at Patrick's high school in New Jersey. The shows were great, and they were more than halfway done with their East Coast tour. After the performance, they loaded back into the two cars and were on their way to their next stops. The guys knew better than to bombard one host with the entire group, so they had decided to sleep in two different places.

Cruising along the freeway, the guys drove past a coffee shop. In front, there was an enormous sign with "We Have Donuts" emblazoned on it. In a decision that feels obvious to a group of college guys who loved *The Simpsons*, they had to have the sign. Both cars pulled off the highway, and with no plan and nothing but a single pocket knife, they tried to liberate the sign. Simple enough, Charlie thought. However, at that very moment, the staff from the coffee shop (one of them being "a big dude" in Charlie's words) realized what was going on and ran out of the store toward the group. The guys all panicked, and scattered to avoid getting in trouble.

Randy took off immediately with the guys who were already in his car, fleeing the scene and hoping to get away without trouble, specifically trying to not involve his father's car. Steve waited for a few members to clamber into his car, and then they were gone, too. Jerome and Charlie were the last guys standing.

The crew from the coffee shop got closer and closer, urging Charlie and Jerome to stay put. His hands were up in the air as he said, "Don't run, don't run, guys." But run is exactly what Jerome did. With Jerome gone, Charlie and the coffee shop crew member faced off. Charlie knew he had a slim chance of negotiating his way out of this situation: they had tried to take the sign, and they had been caught. There wasn't much left to debate. But he saw one flicker of hope. After Jerome was just out of reach, Charlie saw that the coffee crew had a split-second decision to make. They could chase after Jerome, or focus on Charlie.

CHARLIE MECHLING

Straight No Chaser talking with fans after their April 2018 show in Lancaster, Pennsylvania. The guys do a signing line after every show, as they love to meet with Chasers any chance they get. *Credit: Josh Adams*

Charlie never gave them the chance to make that choice. In that split second, Jerome had shouted for Charlie to run. Charlie later learned that Jerome had spotted one of the Straight No Chaser cars, which had fled the scene but later parked on top of a small hill on the other side of the highway.

"All I heard was '*Yo, Charlie! Run, Charlie, run!*' and so I turned and sprinted as fast as I could away from that place. All I knew is that I didn't want to call my parents from jail."

Charlie had youth and athleticism on his side. He ran as fast as he could and dove into the waiting car. They peeled out, laughing and soaked with sweat from the adrenaline and relief that they had gotten away. They decided to just continue on with their plan, so Walt, Jerome, Dan, and DR drove off in Steve's car to stay at Walt's parents' house, and the rest of the guys headed to Patrick's house for the night in Randy's SUV. They planned to reunite at Walt's high school the next day.

The next morning, Charlie, Randy, Patrick, and Steve pulled up at the high school and expected to meet the other half of the group for a quick preshow rehearsal. They hadn't seen or talked to the guys since the day before. It was the pre–cell phone days (remember those?). When the high school administrators started to get antsy about the show, the guys started making phone calls. They called Walt's parents' house, called Patrick's parents' house, and learned nothing of the location of the other four guys. Meanwhile, hundreds of high school students sat impatiently waiting for this a cappella group featuring one of their own alumni to perform at their assembly.

Without any information and no clue how to explain it, Charlie and his crew called the show off. They only had three basses and a tenor present, and there was no way they could make the show work. They apologized to the school. And with that, the East Coast Tour ended early, and the tour became the singular East Coast Gig.

Want to know where the other car went? Get Walt's side of the story in Part Two in chapter 6. *Spoiler alert: the guys weren't done with the donut sign yet!*

An Almost Common-Law Marriage

There's nothing like a brotherly romance. Charlie and Steve have the ultimate bromance, and during their early Straight No Chaser years, they lived together for so long that they qualified for most common-law marriage requirements. The clock started ticking when Steve, Charlie, and Walt became roommates their senior year at Indiana University. Their first three years together had been nearly side by side with evening rehearsals, summers in Chicago, spring break trips, and weekend performances. Why not make things official and move in together?

CHARLIE MECHLING

SNC M&C

Main Course

SERVES 8

DR and Steve added their spin to this recipe while they were living in NYC. Fellow IU a cappella alumni were dining at DR and Steve's humble Upper West Side apartment before seeing the collegiate group (including Tyler and Seggie) perform at Lincoln Center. As the story goes, they wanted to impress their visitors, so they took inspiration from a local restaurant's "family meal" recipe and then added "a little more of everything!" Just like that, the SNC M&C was created.

PREP: 15 MINUTES   **COOK: 40 MINUTES**

INGREDIENTS

1 package (16 ounces) elbow macaroni

3 cups heavy cream

2 ½ cups grated sharp yellow cheddar cheese

1 onion, minced

3 cloves garlic, minced

1 tablespoon Dijon or stone-ground mustard

4 teaspoon Worcestershire sauce

3 teaspoon Tabasco sauce

2 teaspoon ground black pepper

⅓ cup grated parmesan

⅓ cup fine bread crumbs

INSTRUCTIONS

Preheat oven to 400°F.

Bring a large stockpot of water to boil. Add a healthy helping of kosher or coarse salt (the water should taste like the sea).

Add macaroni and cook for 5–6 minutes, until flexible but very al dente. Drain, then let macaroni stand in a colander and under cool water until chilled (this is especially important if using gluten free pasta). Drain fully, then set aside.

In a saucepan, add 1 tablespoon of olive oil over medium-high heat. Once hot (check this by sprinkling water into the pan; if it pops, it's right). Add onion and cook for 5 minutes, then add minced garlic. Cook until the onion is translucent.

Add heavy cream to the saucepan and bring to a boil, still over medium-high heat. Once boiling, reduce heat to low and stir in the cheddar, mustard, Worcestershire, Tabasco, and salt to taste. Stir over low heat until the cheese is completely melted. Remove the pan and adjust the flavor as you see fit; it should have a strong taste at this point.

Add cheese mixture to the pasta. Allow this to cool completely; you can even do this the day before.

Once the pasta and cheese are cooled completely, make sure they are fully incorporated together; the cheese should really stick to the pasta. Mix the parmesan cheese and bread crumbs together and sprinkle over the pasta mix. Cook 30–40 minutes, until the sauce is bubbling and the top is golden brown and crusty.

The fact that Charlie, Steve, and Walt decided to be roommates is a quick glimpse into what it means to be part of Straight No Chaser. It's truly a brotherhood. Even when the members could choose to live with other people and build in some space from the other guys, they didn't. Rather, they decided to spend even more time together. The friendships came easy. Their interests aligned, and they all took music seriously, but they didn't take themselves too seriously. The camaraderie on stage that Chasers everywhere experience doesn't end when a performance is over. In fact, it's the opposite. The banter and energy on stages exists *because* of the friendships offstage.

For Charlie and Steve, that friendship is decades strong and growing.

In 1999, five of the original Straight No Chaser members graduated and moved on from Indiana University. Charlie, Dan, Mike (Itkoff), Steve, and Jerome ended their time with the collegiate group, but no one wanted to end their time as singers and performers. They had a vision of being a five-man group, not too unlike the popular boy bands at the time. The group they formed, called Ten to Five, hallmarked the members' graduation from the ten-man Straight No Chaser. After a quick post-graduation hiatus in Indianapolis where Steve and Charlie lived together, they reunited with Jerome, Dan, and Mike in Atlanta to pursue a record deal with RCA in 2000.

Then September 11, 2001, happened. The national tragedy seemed to impact nearly every industry, including the music industry. Record sales dropped across the industry. Tours were canceled or postponed, and benefit concerts sprang up in their place. Artists, labels, and producers needed time to consider how their music was impacting people. Then, in late September 2001, the Recording Industry Association of America's copyright infringement case against Napster was partially settled in courts. It was a big month in the music industry, and the RCA agreement with Ten to Five ended.

Charlie and Steve saw this change in plans as an opportunity to move forward with their own futures, and they both wanted to head to New York to pursue musical theater. They continued their three-year streak as roommates and decided to rent a tiny apartment in Astoria, Queens, where they ended up living for the next few years.

In New York, Charlie and Steve did everything they could to make their dream of being Broadway performers come to life. They both worked in catering and as bartenders, two of the hottest industries for aspiring performers due to the flexibility. They worked to pay the bills and auditioned as often as they could. It wasn't uncommon for meals to be leftover food from catering events or to stock their shelves with extra bottles of alcohol that "would have been thrown out anyway" (debatable). Eventually, the guys amassed the largest at-home bar selection of any of their friends. Charlie also got used to eating Steve's cooking with whatever they could afford at the time, calling their favorite hearty, budget-friendly meals "Indiana fancy."

They made their way as performers, picking up roles in national tours like Seussical. Both Charlie and Steve got roles in the musical, as did a third friend from IU, Jon Armstrong. They made it work, and it worked out.

That is, until they fell in love. Not with each other, but each with their future wives. Charlie met his wife, Julia, while living with Steve. Julia, a performer, was also working in catering at the time. Charlie likes to joke that Julia killed his relationship with Steve, but he knew the night that he met Julia, he never wanted to let her go.

Steve had also met his future wife, Emily, while they were working on the same show. Ultimately, Charlie and Steve knew that love would win out, and their common-law marriage came to a bittersweet end.

Go Ask Your Mom

Collingswood, New Jersey, 2012. Any Straight No Chaser fan who attended this particular concert will know the exact power of one of Charlie's favorite moments of any live performance in their career.

The group was booked to perform at a Masonic temple. The temple was busy that evening; a senior prom was taking place on the lower level, and Straight No Chaser was performing directly above them. The room was beautiful: open, full of stone, high ceilings, and filled with fans, eager to hear the show. Everything started out great: the guys had their wireless microphones and earpieces on like they do at most shows. They started singing their set, and quickly realized that the evening's performance was not going to be typical. By the third song, their microphones started dropping in and out. They noticed that their in-ear

LEMON ORZO SHRIMP

Main Course

SERVES 4

This one-pot meal would be a perfect dish to serve before attending a Straight No Chaser concert. It's fresh, filling, and ends with a little tang of citrus.

PREP: 15 MINUTES   **COOK: 45 MINUTES**

INGREDIENTS

1 tablespoon vegetable oil

1 large zucchini, cut lengthwise, then into ¼-inch slices

¼ teaspoon salt

4 cloves garlic, finely chopped

¾ cup uncooked orzo pasta

1 ½ cups sodium chicken broth

1 lb. uncooked large shrimp, peeled, deveined, tail shells removed

2 tablespoons butter

¼ cup grated Parmesan cheese

1 teaspoon fresh lemon juice

1 teaspoon fresh thyme leaves, chopped

Heat oil in skillet over medium heat.

Sauté zucchini and salt until zucchini is slightly tender. Remove zucchini from skillet and set aside.

In the same pan over medium heat, add garlic and orzo. Cook until the garlic is fragrant, about 2–3 minutes. Add chicken broth, stir up the mixture, cover and simmer for 10 minutes.

Stir in the shrimp and butter. Add the cooked zucchini back to the skillet. Cook until shrimp are cooked through (pink) and orzo pasta is tender.

Stir in Parmesan cheese, fresh lemon juice, and fresh thyme leaves.

If desired, top with fresh parsley and serve!

SNC High Note: For all the white wine–loving Chasers, this dish goes out to you. Pairs well with overly generous pours.

monitors weren't working consistently either. Charlie remembers making eye contact with the other members, and everyone looked equally confused. The songs started to suffer, and that was not going to work.

The guys called an early intermission and apologized to the audience. They promised to be back and ready to go for the rest of the show with no further interruptions. Backstage, their sound engineer explained the situation. There were police officers monitoring all of the doors at the prom on the lower level. The police transmitters and the frequencies they used completely dominated the atmosphere, and that interference crashed Straight No Chaser's wireless microphones and monitors. There was no way around it. The guys had two options: cancel the show and refund all the tickets, or perform the rest of the show acoustically, without any amplification. As the saying goes, the show must go on. They went back out on stage, explained the situation to the audience, and prepared them for an unplanned, impromptu off-mic performance. Charlie took a deep breath, and the group started singing. They tapped into their earliest days, standing in a semi-circle, projecting their voices to the back of the room, using everything they had to get the notes to carry to all audience members. People were on the edge of their seats, and what Charlie remembers most is how silent and respectful the audience was. No noises, no disruptions. They sat still, giving the group the best chance they had to perform. It was a breathtaking performance and one that Chasers still bring up when they have a chance to talk with Straight No Chaser.

And *that* is how you turn an audience member into a Chaser.

So, what does Straight No Chaser think of their fans, who call themselves Chasers? Pretty much the world. Chasers started out on a high note when they got their nickname from Kathie Lee Gifford on a *Today Show* appearance. She wanted to be one of the first "official" fans of Straight No Chaser, but she wasn't sure what to call herself. She devised her own name: a Chaser. The name stuck. But if you ask Charlie, it's a bit of a misnomer, and Gifford certainly wasn't the first Straight No Chaser fan. Chasers aren't necessarily chasing after Straight No Chaser. At least, not in the "hide-your-face-from-the-paparazzi" celebrity kind of way. It's more of the opposite in Charlie's opinion. The Chasers are what Straight No Chaser is after. Every performance is about making sure the fans get everything they want. Traveling around the world is about seeing friends

CHARLIE MECHLING

and, even better, watching other people become friends through their shared appreciation for Straight No Chaser's music.

Take Rachel, for instance. Rachel is a fan who has been coming to shows since she was eight years old. Now, she's in college (*"She can drive! She can vote!"*) and she's still a fan. Charlie still remembers the bunny that she would bring with her to the shows for all of the guys to sign, and she would draw each member his own picture. That's just the kind of people Chasers are. Rachel might be a bit of an exception on age. In Charlie's words, "Go Ask Your Mom" is the official demographic of Straight No Chaser. Ask someone if they've heard of Straight No Chaser and the answer is no, then tell them, "Go ask your mom. She'll know." Charlie couldn't be prouder of that. He knows that many Chasers are women like his own mom. She is going to enjoy a glass of white wine, grab her husband, and insist that he go to the Straight No Chaser concert with her. And that man, he'll start tapping along. And nodding his head. And appreciating the classic show tunes. After the show, he'll be the first to tell Charlie that he really wasn't expecting to enjoy the show but, hey! He really did!

They'll bring their grandkids to the next show. Those grandkids will giggle at "The Disney Medley" and sing along to the pop songs. And from their phone, right in their seat in the audience, they'll download the album and follow the group on social media. Their mom will hear it at home, and she'll insist on a ticket to the show the next time Straight No Chaser is in town. Suddenly, there's a new family tradition.

All of it is perfect.

The loyalty that Charlie and the other members have experienced from Chasers is unparalleled to anything else they've experienced in life, outside of the support of their own parents. Some of the Chasers have been in the guys' lives for longer than their wives. They are committed to the group. They grieve when members move on from Straight No Chaser, and they welcome new members with open arms and a little bit of tough love to keep them motivated. The Chasers have been around for as long as Straight No Chaser, and it wouldn't surprise Charlie if they stuck around long after, too.

RANDY STINE

Meet the Bloomingtones

Imagine a world in which your favorite a cappella group was the Bloomingtones. Or that you're treating the grandchildren to a night out with Levels. In the fall of 1996, during their first two weeks as a group, both of these names were on the short list. Randy Stine contributed a few name ideas, including Straight No Chaser, which he read off the back of the 1967 Thelonious Monk album of the same name, *Straight, No Chaser.* Randy was taking Jazz Studies with the late distinguished professor David Baker at the time and had grown to so appreciate Monk's work that he went to the local Borders Bookstore and bought several of the classic albums. The guys debated many name suggestions, but the general reaction to all the name options was a collective shrug, and the newly formed group remained nameless for their first few weeks.

A split-second decision during their first public performance determined their moniker. It was October 1996, and the guys had been up since 3 a.m., preparing for their 7 a.m. timeslot at IU's Dance Marathon. They met at the local Denny's to plan the set list, discuss the group names, and grab something to eat. They even squeezed in one final rehearsal in the hallway outside of the Indiana Memorial Union, before heading to the HPER building for the event. Excitedly, the guys walked onto stage, Dan Ponce brought his microphone to his mouth and said, "Hey everyone! We are . . ." He turned back toward the guys and asked, "What name are we going with?" Dan needed an answer. Charlie whispered loudly, "Straight No Chaser!"

Dan returned to his microphone. "We are . . . Straight No Chaser!"

And just that like, the group had their name. Straight No Chaser was now, officially, IU's newest a cappella group.

Randy is one of the founding members of Straight No Chaser. Randy sang in several a cappella groups in high school but hadn't found anything similar to join on campus. He began searching for a music faculty member to help him create a professor-led a cappella group. At the start of his sophomore year, he joined the Singing Hoosiers, where he met Dan Ponce. They bonded over their Chicago roots and their desire for a university a cappella group.

Randy is proud of the way the original group formed. All of the guys had to formally audition to be in the Singing Hoosiers, so the level of vocal talent was already high. The defining characteristics of someone asked to join SNC was their musical skill, followed closely by their ability to get along with all the other members. There was something about this group of guys that felt right to Randy. Jerome, Steve, Charlie, Dan, DR, Walt, Mike, Kevin, and Patrick were talented vocalists. Their strong work ethic, and passion for performing gave the group an early advantage. Their chemistry and humor made the friendships come easy.

The name worked for the group. It was clever and fun, and it had a nice connection to the a cappella style of singing (straight up) with no instruments (chaser.) It's also a phrase tied to alcohol, which clashed with the university's dry campus policy. When the group performed at official Indiana University events, the university would change their name in the printed program to, simply, "Men's Ensemble."

However, the group knew they were onto something: sororities and fraternities were requesting them to sing at their campus events, as well

The past and present members of Straight No Chaser perform a song together at the IU Auditorium in December 2018. Left to right: Walter Chase, Mike Itkoff, Tyler Trepp, Don Nottingham, Randy Stine, Dan Ponce, Jerome Collins, Ryan Ahlwardt, Mike Luginbill, David Roberts, Seggie Isho, Steve Morgan, and Charlie Mechling. *Credit: Evan De Stefano Photography*

ART SMITH'S FRIED CHICKEN

Main Course

SERVES 4

The connection between Straight No Chaser and Art Smith is a great story. During the 2010 summer run at Harrah's Casino in Atlantic City, Randy was sitting in a booth with the group's manager, David Britz, when David looked up from his laptop and asked, "Do you know who Chef Art Smith is?"

Randy immediately knew. Art Smith was Oprah's personal chef and a successful restaurateur.

"He wants to know if Straight No Chaser can sing at his wedding," David said. One month later, Straight No Chaser performed at Chef Art's wedding to his partner, Jesus, in front of more than four hundred guests at Smith's Art and Soul restaurant on Capitol Hill in Washington, DC.

This began a lifelong friendship, with Chef Art and his family attending many SNC shows, hosting SNC at his restaurants, and even throwing an afterparty for the guys at his private home after a two-show day at the Chicago Theatre. Being nearby in Chicago, Randy still regularly catches up with Chef Art and brings his wife and family into his restaurants for delicious meals. Thanks to the generosity of Chef Art, we are able to feature his world-famous recipes in our collection!

PREP: 48 HOURS (TWO OVERNIGHTS) + 30 MINUTES   **COOK: 30 MINUTES**

INGREDIENTS

1 whole chicken, cut into pieces (thighs, legs, wings, backs), trimmed of any excess skin

½ cup salt

Enough water to cover chicken by 1 inch

Enough buttermilk to just cover chicken (approx. 4 cups)

2 tablespoons Tabasco

2 cups all-purpose flour

1 teaspoon kosher salt

1 tablespoon baking powder

1 ½ teaspoons garlic powder

1 ½ teaspoons Old Bay Seasoning

1 teaspoon cayenne pepper

1 teaspoon freshly ground black pepper

Vegetable oil, for frying

In a pot, dissolve the ½ cup of salt in the water; submerge the chicken in the brine; refrigerate overnight.

Drain and rinse the chicken; rinse out the pot; add the buttermilk and hot sauce, submerge the chicken in the buttermilk and refrigerate for 8 hours or overnight.

In a shallow bowl, mix the flour, baking powder, garlic powder, Old Bay, cayenne, black pepper, and the remaining 1 teaspoon of salt.

Run your fingers down each piece of chicken to remove excess buttermilk, then dredge in the flour; dip the chicken back into the buttermilk and coat again in the flour.

Meanwhile, in a large cast-iron skillet, heat 1 inch of vegetable oil to 350–365°F; fry the chicken in batches until golden and cooked through, about 6 minutes per side.

Drain on paper towels and keep warm in a preheated oven at 250°F until ready to serve.

as their mom's or dad's weekends. The guys were handling their marketing with hands-on effort: chalking sidewalks around the campus, hanging up flyers, and even surprising dorm residents by going floor to floor, knocking on doors and singing down the hallways. Their first on-campus concert had more than nine hundred people in attendance. The university took notice.

Senior year, Randy got a call from the head of the IU Alumni Association, asking for him to come in and have a meeting. His first thoughts were trouble: *Did we chalk in a restricted area? Who is failing a class?* The reality was the opposite. The President and CEO had seen Straight No Chaser perform live at a wedding rehearsal dinner; they were hooked, and they wanted to sponsor the group officially. They offered the group an office in the alumni building, a telephone line, and administrative support. The Alumni Association wanted to tap into the talents of Straight No Chaser and send them to fundraising events on behalf of the university. The tables had turned. Straight No Chaser was officially on the program.

Randy the Cameraman

Randy's father got their family's first camcorder when Randy was in junior high, but it ended up in Randy's hands more often than anyone else's. He had dreams of working in movie and television production. He admired directors like Steven Spielberg, and he was obsessed with comedy and the production of *Saturday Night Live*. He produced short films with friends and convinced teachers to allow him to submit videos in place of assignments. He used humor in his videos to get laughs from the class while sneaking in lessons about the Pythagorean theorem and paramecium. Randy loved being the reason that teachers would roll the big AV cart out of the corner of the classroom—an event that anyone over the age of thirty can appreciate.

Randy's love for production was always combined with his love of music. He recalls sitting in front of the television at the age of five, recording the audio from Michael Jackson and Huey Lewis music videos onto his Fisher Price tape recorder. Music videos were enchanting to Randy, who was mesmerized by the visualizations of the music that he loved. He appreciated that the visuals could elevate a song, and how certain songs made it impossible not to dance.

Randy tries to get the group's lighting technician, Joe Wine, to demonstrate his vocal chops off stage just before the show begins, October 2019. *Credit: Evan De Stefano Photography*

The line from his childhood hobbies of music and videography made a direct connection to his work with Straight No Chaser. Sidewalk chalk and flyers were raising the group's visibility on campus, but Randy thought the group humor he enjoyed in rehearsals would help win over their audience even more. Randy borrowed his family's camcorder to record behind-the-scenes footage and scripted videos to show the audience before concerts and during intermission.

RANDY'S MARGARITA

Cocktail

Randy put down his camcorder long enough to come up with a delicious personal spin on a classic margarita.

INGREDIENTS

2 ounces (100% agave) Blanco Tequila

1 ounce fresh-squeezed lime juice

1 ounce honey syrup

HONEY SYRUP

Mix equal parts honey and hot (but not boiling) water, then stir to incorporate.

You can make 8–16 ounces in advance, and store it in a sealed container, refrigerated, for up to a month.

Honey syrup can be used the same way simple syrup is used.

COCKTAIL

Fill cocktail shaker with ice.

Pour tequila, lime juice, and honey syrup into shaker.

Shake vigorously for ten seconds.

Pour into a glass with ice.

Garnish with a lime wedge.

SNC High Note: This would be equally delicious as a nonalcoholic beverage. Simply swap the tequila for sparkling water or club soda, shake, and enjoy!

The group never took themselves too seriously, and that helped attract fans from the start. In the somewhat stolid world of a cappella in the mid-1990s, self-deprecating wittiness was a differentiator.

Randy created video treatments for the group, specifically focusing on each member to feature their humor and personality. One member, Mark, was known to be an outdoorsman, so Randy put together a video of him carrying his canoe throughout the campus, including through the student union, eventually canoeing the river on campus and ending up in IU's iconic Showalter Fountain. Another member, Don, worked at a campus pizza spot. Randy created a sequence of him preparing for what seemed like a big date, but the final shot revealed it was just a pizza delivery. Even the president of the university agreed to appear on camera, teaching the guys how to play basketball in one of the videos shown at a campus concert.

Randy has amassed hundreds of hours of Straight No Chaser footage over the years. Most of it still sits in boxes in his basement, but one very important video made it out of storage. It's the one video that changed Randy's and the rest of Straight No Chaser's lives forever.

From Betamax to YouTube

The year 2006 marked the tenth anniversary of the founding of Straight No Chaser. In ten years, Straight No Chaser had gone from a self-formed, on-campus group to a legacy tradition with their own office space at Indiana University. For the ten year reunion show, the university asked the original members to come back, connect with the collegiate group, and sing a few songs. Though the original members had been apart for years, coming back together felt natural and easy.

Back in 1998, Randy petitioned the group to spend $1500 on a three-camera video crew, to document their biggest campus concert to date, at the Musical

In October 1997, just a year after their inception, the group poses during their first-ever photo shoot. Their debut album, *SNC*, featured photos from this shoot. *Courtesy IU Archives.*

ART SMITH'S AUNTIE'S CHOCOLATE CAKE WITH CHOCOLATE-PECAN FROSTING

Dessert

SERVES 12

Chef Art Smith notes that this particular chocolate cake was his Aunt Evelyn's recipe. She loved to cook "portable" foods, and this cake can be easily transported right in the pan to wherever you want to eat it!

PREP: 30 MINUTES   **COOK: 35 MINUTES**

CAKE

2 cups all-purpose flour

2 cups granulated sugar

1 teaspoon baking soda

Pinch of salt

8 tablespoons (1 stick) unsalted butter, cut up

8 tablespoons (1 stick) margarine, cut up

1 cup water

⅓ cup unsweetened cocoa powder (not Dutch process)

¾ cup sour cream

2 large eggs

1 teaspoon vanilla extract

FROSTING

8 tablespoons (1 stick) unsalted butter, cut up

⅓ cup plus 1 tablespoon milk

¼ cup unsweetened cocoa powder (not Dutch process)

1 pound (about 4 ⅓ cups) confectioners' sugar, sifted

1 teaspoon vanilla extract

1 cup (4 ounces) coarsely chopped pecans, toasted

INSTRUCTIONS

CAKE

Position a rack in the center of the oven and preheat to 350°F.

Lightly butter and flour a 13 × 9-inch baking pan, tapping out the excess flour.

Whisk the flour, granulated sugar, baking soda, and salt in a large bowl to combine.

In a medium saucepan, bring the butter, margarine, water and cocoa to a boil over high heat, stirring to dissolve the butter and margarine.

Pour into the flour mixture and whisk well.

Add the sour cream, then the eggs and vanilla, and beat well.

Spread evenly in the pan. Bake until the cake springs back when pressed in the center, about 35 minutes.

Remove from the oven and place on a wire rack.

FROSTING

Bring the butter, milk and cocoa to a boil in a large saucepan over medium heat, stirring to dissolve the butter.

Gradually stir in the confectioners' sugar, then the vanilla.

Stir in the chopped pecans.

Pour over the warm cake. Cool the cake in the pan on the rack.

Cut into pieces and serve directly from the pan.

Straight No Chaser performing "Indiana Christmas," an original song by Dan Ponce, from their debut album *Holiday Spirits*. The group rarely performs this song outside the state of Indiana, and it is all the more special to the guys when they perform it at the IU Auditorium, as in this photo from December 2019. *Credit: Evan De Stefano Photography*

Arts Center. It was also the first time that the group was trying out a new arrangement of their song "The 12 Days of Christmas." Unfortunately, the company they hired went out of business shortly after the concert, and it wasn't until three years later that Randy tracked the owner down and got them to send him the original Betamax tapes. By this time, this video format was nearly obsolete, so it took time to convert the tapes to digital files, and then re-sync them with audio. Five years later, with the reunion looming, Randy wanted to celebrate the anniversary by digging into the hours of collegiate concert footage that he had. He thought it would be a great way to honor the founding of the group and inspire the current members to keep singing together and building the SNC legacy.

Unfortunately for Randy, he had been laid off from his job in IT, but he saw this as an opportunity, because he suddenly had time on his hands. Without this gift of time, he never would have had a schedule that would have allowed him to assemble these videos from years ago. He spent weeks editing, as working with video on a PC in 2006 resulted in many rendering hours and crashes. He slept in his office at his condo, feet from the computer so he could wake up every few hours to click "ok" and render the next segment. Once he was finished with all the editing, he wanted to share the footage with the guys but didn't yet know how to send video over the internet. Randy's friend Greg told him he should try a new site called YouTube, and it was exactly what he was looking for. YouTube had launched in February 2005, and Randy took advantage of the relatively new platform. He uploaded some of concert footage, including "The 12 Days of Christmas" from the original group's 1998 performance, sharing the links with family, friends, and all the guys before the ten-year reunion.

Randy periodically checked his YouTube channel for comments from friends. After eighteen months, the "12 Days of Christmas" video had amassed 100k views ("We thought that was crazy!"). Then, over three weeks in December 2007, the video went viral and topped over seven million views. That tipped the scales, and the video's popularity garnered attention from people around the world. Randy received phone calls from media outlets about the video. The questions were largely about the video itself: how did Randy make it go viral? How did the views spike so suddenly? According to the (now defunct) viralvideochart.com website, "The 12 Days of Christmas" was the most viral video of 2007, and it hit that mark in just the final three weeks of the year. Randy knew that the secret to the video's success was the performance itself. Straight No Chaser's rendition of "The 12 Days of Christmas" took people by surprise.

The original "12 Days of Christmas" arrangement by Richard Gregory had an abrupt ending. Dan Ponce brought the song to the group during a rehearsal and pitched it as a potential song to sing, but the ending left the group wanting more. Straight No Chaser had just decided to finally retire Toto's "Africa" from their set list. It had been a part of their shows since the beginning, and the guys had grown tired of singing it at every single show for the past three years. Charlie, in particular, was ready to move on and cut "Africa." Randy, poking fun at Charlie, joked that they could just end "12 Days" with "Africa." However, that joke turned into a real idea for Dan Ponce, who returned to the next rehearsal after the Thanksgiving break with the arrangement transitioning into "Africa," complete with holiday-themed lyrics. It sounded good, made the guys laugh, and most importantly the fans would love the inside joke that "Africa" would still be included in the show. That was the performance that went viral.

The early interjections of various Christmas songs kept people interested from the start, but the surprise transition to "Africa" is the main reason Randy thinks people decided to share the video with their family and friends, making the song viral. Connections started pouring in. Bob Lefsetz, a prominent music blogger, wrote a piece on Straight No Chaser's viral video. Steve Luthaker, the guitarist from Toto, reached out to Randy to talk about the song. Mark Cuban emailed Randy about the group potentially reuniting for a special on HDNet. The attention was fun and flattering, but nothing major came of it. Randy didn't think much about a YouTube message from a cryptic username, who said they were with Atlantic Records, but he shared his phone number anyway, just to explore a conversation with the record label. He expected it to be a conversation similar to the others he had about licensing the song.

On New Year's Day in 2008, Randy received a call from Craig Kallman, the Chariman and CEO of Atlantic Records. Randy couldn't believe it. He actually wondered if it was a friend changing their voice to play a prank. Craig Kallman was very real, and he invited Randy to join him in Los Angeles for dinner to talk about the future of Straight No Chaser.

Straight No Chaser Meets Atlantic Records

Randy had quit another a cappella group in Chicago, due to their lack of focus, preparation, and professionalism. He said to a friend, "The only way I would do a cappella again is if SNC somehow got back together." The call from Craig Kallman of Atlantic Records was a dream come true. Ever since he finished college and left the collegiate group, Randy dreamed of somehow reuniting the group, to perform again. It's what motivated him to spend hours digitizing old Betamax tapes into digital files in the spring of 2006. It motivated him to share the group's performance videos on YouTube. So when Randy's phone rang on January 1, 2008, and the chairman and CEO of Atlantic Records asked Randy to fly to LA for dinner, he was ready to go.

Randy called Dan Ponce right away: "What's your schedule this week? Get out of work. We're going to LA."

The worst case scenario was that the two guys got a free trip to LA and no record deal. The best case scenario was what Randy had always hoped for: a chance to make SNC happen in the big leagues.

A stretch limousine picked up Randy and Dan in LA and took them directly to the Peninsula Hotel. From the moment they walked in, the guys knew they had walked into an entirely different world. Actress Diane Keaton was next to them at check in. Michael Jackson and Britney Spears were also guests at the hotel that night, so the place was crawling with paparazzi, and Randy and Dan stuck out like sore thumbs. That night, they met Craig Kallman and Jesse Ignjatovic, the producer of the MTV Video Music Awards, for dinner at Spago, the Wolfgang Puck restaurant in Beverly Hills. Randy and Dan arrived ready for a midwestern business meeting. They walked in dressed head to toe in full suits, not realizing that Los Angeles does everything low-key, including eating at Spago in jeans

ART SMITH'S HUMMINGBIRD CAKE

Dessert

SERVES 12

Hummingbird Cake is a southern specialty. It features banana, pineapple, and pecans in a spice cake, and is typically served with a thick cream cheese frosting. Chef Art supplied each SNC tour bus with their own Hummingbird Cake when they played Chicago!

PREP: 20 MINUTES   **COOK: 30 MINUTES + 1 HOUR COOLING TIME**

CAKE

3 cups all-purpose flour
2 cups granulated sugar
1 teaspoon baking soda
1 teaspoon ground cinnamon
½ teaspoon salt
2 cups chopped ripe bananas
1 cup drained crushed pineapple
1 cup vegetable oil
2 large eggs, beaten
1 ½ teaspoons vanilla extract
1 cup (4 ounces) finely chopped pecans

ICING

8 ounces cream cheese, at room temperature
½ cup (1 stick) butter, at room temperature
1 pound confectioners' sugar (about 4 ½ cups sifted)
1 teaspoon vanilla extract

INSTRUCTIONS

CAKE

Preheat oven to 350°F and position racks in the center and bottom third of the oven.

Lightly butter two 9-inch round cake pans, sprinkle evenly with flour, and tap out the excess. If you wish, butter the pans, line the bottoms with rounds of parchment paper, then flour the pans and tap out the excess.

Sift the flour, sugar, baking soda, cinnamon, and salt into a bowl.

In another bowl, stir or whisk the bananas, pineapple, oil, eggs, and vanilla until combined. Do not use an electric mixer.

Pour into the dry mixture and fold together with a large spatula just until smooth. Do not beat. Fold in the pecans. Spread evenly into the pans.

Bake until the cake springs back when pressed in the center, 30–35 minutes.

Transfer the cakes to wire racks and cool for 10 minutes. Invert the cakes onto the racks (remove the parchment paper now if using). Turn right side up and cool completely for at least one hour.

ICING

Using an electric mixer on high speed, beat the cream cheese and butter in a large bowl until combined.

On low speed, gradually beat in the sugar, then the vanilla, to make a smooth icing.

Place 1 cake layer upside down on a serving platter; spread with about ⅔ cup of the icing.

Top with the second layer, right side up.

Spread the remaining icing over the top and sides of the cake.

The cake can be prepared up to 1 day ahead and stored, uncovered, in the refrigerator.

Let stand at room temperature 1 hour before serving.

and T-shirts. It was their record-scratch moment, as everyone in the restaurant looked at them, correctly, as if to say, "They aren't from here." They sat down at the table, and Jesse Ignatovic pulled out a binder of details. In addition to a record deal, MTV wanted Straight No Chaser for a reality-style television series. Randy and Dan listened and asked questions.

Atlantic Records wanted a record deal, but they wanted all of Straight No Chaser to come to New York to perform at their headquarters to get everyone on the same page. Randy and Dan knew it wasn't their decision alone to make. They went back to the Peninsula Hotel Bar and came up with a plan. They would go back to Chicago, and together they would call each one of the guys to tell them about this incredible opportunity. They began their phone calls casually, catching up with each member before giving them the news. Call by call, each member flipped out. Jerome, who was in Hong Kong at the time, was the only member who couldn't make it to the meeting.

The trip to New York served as a mini reunion for the group. It was fun under any circumstance to be back together as Straight No Chaser, but it was even better when the meeting of a lifetime is on the agenda. The night before the meeting, they got dinner, caught up, and rehearsed for the next day. In the morning, they went to Atlantic Records' Sixth Avenue office building and were escorted to the conference room. Craig Kallman was there, as well as about fifteen other Atlantic Records executives and staff.

Despite their nerves, the guys sang their hearts out. Randy caught a glimpse of Kallman, who had a thoughtful look on his face, but in the middle of singing, the CEO abruptly stood up and left the room. The group's collective heart sank. They thought for sure they had blown it, and that Kallman was over his initial excitement about the group. Then, the door opened, and he walked back in, this time with two additional people with him.

"Okay guys. This is a go. If you don't have an agent, go get one. I want a contract worked out by next week. We need to move quickly if we're going to have a Christmas album ready for release this fall."

Trying to play it cool, the guys shook a few hands, made a bit of small talk, and kept their excitement hidden as they made their way to the door. Once they left the building, the guys burst into excitement, jumping up and down on Avenue of the Americas. They bought bottles of champagne and called their families to share the news: Atlantic Records wanted to sign Straight No Chaser. Weeks later, on a return trip to New York, the guys signed the official contract, celebrated, and promptly left the signed contract at a bar. Luckily the responsible bar owner allowed the guys to get it back and return the completed document to the label the next day.

That first few months as a professional group, Randy and the guys commuted back and forth to New York every weekend to rehearse roughly twenty songs in preparation for their first album. They kept their day jobs, working five days a week, flying to New York on Friday, rehearsing all day Saturday and Sunday, then taking the last flight home. The schedule was intense and exhausting, but it was worth it. The first professional album, *Holiday Spirits*, was recorded in just two weeks at AirTime Studios in Bloomington, Indiana, where the group had recorded some of their college albums as well. Their debut album became the number-one selling album on both the iTunes and Amazon charts on December 22, 2008.

Walt sings to a Bloomington, Indiana, crowd in 2017.
Credit: Evan De Stefano Photography

WALTER CHASE

The Name's Chase, Walter Chase.

Walter Chase hasn't always been Walter Chase. He was born Walter Shilanskas. Growing up north of Philadelphia in Easton, Pennsylvania, Walt was a musical kid. He sang in church during elementary school. He started doing musicals in the sixth grade. He developed a love for choir during high school, and eventually became president of his choir. Walt even started his own high school a cappella group with friends. By the time he was a junior, his life plan was to take over his beloved choir teacher's job. In his own words, Walt was obsessed. His trajectory toward becoming an original member of Straight No Chaser is about as on-brand as you can get.

Walt joined Straight No Chaser the year it was formed, which was his sophomore year. That same week, he was accepted into Delusions of Grandeur, a six-man comedic a cappella group. As a self-described bunch of clowns who had a lot of fun, Delusions of Grandeur was Walt's counterbalance to Straight No Chaser. He loved being goofy and having fun with Delusions of Grandeur, but he knew that Straight No Chaser had more potential. It was polished and popular, and much more musically tight.

Walt went to Indiana University to study music education, intent on becoming a teacher. At one point, Walt was simultaneously doing his student teaching, directing a musical on campus, and singing with Straight No Chaser and Delusions of Grandeur. During that time, he learned three very important things about himself. First, he realized that he lacked both the patience and the focus to be the kind of teacher that he wanted to be. Second, he learned that he had an incredible talent for making musical arrangements. Third, a cappella was his life. His realizations confirmed what he suspected about his future in education: being a teacher in the traditional sense just didn't strike the right chord for him. Walt felt he was skilled at teaching in different ways, like directing musical arrangements and groups of vocalists, so he shifted all of his energy towards his a cappella groups.

His obsession with a cappella groups, particularly Straight No Chaser, served him well. Walt enjoyed teaching vocalists, and he loved making arrangements for SNC. But he didn't have the swagger that he saw in other performers (let's be honest, it's Jerome) and the confidence that came with it. As Walt put more and more energy into his friendships within the group, he got more and more out of it. Walt loved Straight No Chaser; the group became his entire social scene, and most of his time revolved around the group's schedule. Walt remembers watching Jerome perform and win people over with his charisma and stage presence. Straight No Chaser is, above all, a brotherhood, and no one guy stood alone. Walt recalls how generously the other guys would share the stage, giving highlights and space for Walt to step up every time he was ready. He learned from Jerome's social cues and took note of Dan's leadership skills. He saw the confidence they carried and felt that they earned every drop of it. Walt absorbed everything. Straight No Chaser gave Walt the space, friends, and opportunity to be exactly who he wanted to be.

Walt found his place in the group where he could be his best and make an impact. It was his exchange for riding the coattails of confidence the other guys provided to him. Walt could put musical arrangements together quickly, and he had an ear for creating smooth transitions. He loved to be behind the scenes, working through the nuances of a program to make sure the onstage performance worked. He thrived as the producer, but he didn't shy away from the opportunity to sing on stage. After a fifth year at Indiana University taking graduate courses and exploring potential career paths, Walt quit pretending that his future was going to be anything other than music. He packed up his things,

Seggie, Walt, and Steve performing "Do You Hear What I Hear" during a holiday set in Pittsburgh, December 2017. *Credit: Mitch Straub*

scrapped plans to pursue a graduate degree, and moved on to the next chapter of his life.

For three years, Walt lived in State College, Pennsylvania, and worked as a musician in a band called Seven Souls. The group played primarily cover songs, and they worked their way around the mid-Atlantic region. Walt liked the thrill of being a performer and supporting the direction of the group. More performances meant more stage time and more introductions. For Walt, this

SAUSAGE, SAUERKRAUT, MUSTARD BASE PIZZA WITH HOMEMADE CRUST

Main Course

SERVES 12

Walt hails from an Italian family. Pizza has been a staple food in his life for as long as he can remember. His love for food earned him the Straight No Chaser nickname of Fatty (said with love, of course).

PREP: 35 MINUTES + 30 MINUTES   **RISING TIME FOR DOUGH**   **COOK: 35 MINUTES**

DOUGH

2–2 ⅓ cups all-purpose flour, divided

1 packet instant yeast

1 ½ teaspoons sugar

¾ teaspoon salt

⅛–¼ teaspoon garlic powder

2 tablespoons olive oil + additional

¾ cup warm water

Preheat oven to 425°F.

Combine 1 cup of flour, yeast, sugar, salt, and garlic powder in a large bowl.

Add olive oil and warm water and use a wooden spoon to stir very well.

Gradually add another 1 cup of flour. Add any additional flour as needed until the dough forms into an elastic ball and pulls away from the sides.

Drizzle a separate, large, clean bowl generously with olive oil and use a pastry brush to brush the sides of the bowl.

Dust hands with flour. Mold your dough into a ball and transfer to the prepared bowl; roll dough around until coated with oil; cover the bowl with plastic wrap and place in a warm spot to rise for 30 minutes or until doubled in size.

Remove risen dough and use your hands to gently deflate it and transfer to a lightly floured surface; knead a few times until the dough is smooth.

Form the dough into a 12-inch circle using your hands or a floured rolling pin.

Line a pizza pan with parchment paper and transfer dough; pinch or fold edges to form a crust.

Drizzle an additional tablespoon of olive oil on the pizza crust and spread evenly with a pastry brush; poke small holes in the dough, avoiding the crust, to prevent dough from bubbling.

Add toppings (see below).

TOPPINGS

1 teaspoon of fennel seeds

½ cup stone ground mustard

1 teaspoon apple cider vinegar

½–¾ lbs. sausage, cooked and crumbled

10 ounces sauerkraut

10 ounces shredded gruyere or swiss cheese

Whisk together fennel seeds, ground mustard, and apple cider vinegar.

Spread on prepared pizza crust.

Top with sausage and sauerkraut.

Finish with cheese; distribute evenly across pizza.

Bake in the preheated oven for 15 minutes.

The group bows after the final song of their 2019 show at the IU Auditorium.
Credit: Evan De Stefano Photography

was all exciting except for one unavoidable nuisance: spelling and saying his last name. Making small talk about the challenges of spelling and saying Shilanskas over and over became tedious. For three years, Walt let a name change linger in the back of his mind. What would it be like to take on a different name—and maybe a different persona altogether?

He got the answer when he joined fellow Straight No Chaser alum DR on a cruise ship in 2003. Walt had finished his time with Seven Souls. He was now exploring the world on a cruise ship (a common theme among collegiate Straight No Chaser alum). It was the perfect time to try something new with his audiences. A fresh audience arrived with every cruise, so Walt had the opportunity to play around without losing any major momentum. It didn't take long for Walt to try out one of the names that had been on his mind for years: Chase. Aboard the cruise ship, he started introducing himself as Walter Chase. Straight No Chaser was a huge part of Walt's identity during college, and it felt right to him to absorb part of the group as part of his new name and persona. Some of Walt's best friends in the world were part of that group, and the name Chase was significantly easier than his given name to pronounce. Under the comfort of a cruise ship, Walt tried out the name. It had a ring to it, and that was powerful for Walt. He felt like the name worked for him, and the ease of it felt right. He called up his girlfriend at the time (who is now his wife) and ran the idea past her. She agreed that it was a strong choice, and the decision was set. Walter Shilanskas was no more. From here on out, it would be Chase, Walter Chase.

A Cappella–Friendly

The first summer Walt stayed in Chicago with Straight No Chaser, his car got broken into. The thief smashed a window and grabbed a few handfuls of things from Walt's car. Most were insignificant, but one was major: fifteen different hand-written arrangements across hundreds of pages.

That was so *not* a cappella–friendly.

Being a cappella–friendly is, in fact, a real thing. It's a characteristic of a song that describes its potential for becoming an a cappella arrangement. It's a combination of instrumentation, melody, and harmony. A good indicator of a song's a cappella–friendliness is whether it can be turned into a nice acoustic arrangement. For the Beatles fans out there, John's songs are not a cappella–friendly. They rely on the atmosphere and the attack of sounds. In contrast, Paul's songs are more a cappella–friendly due to their melody and style. It's not a perfect science, but Walt has years of experience, listening for when a song is great for a cappella. When he finds those songs, he goes straight to the drawing board to create a vocals-only arrangement.

That's exactly what Walt was up to when his car got broken into in Chicago. Walt was helping to create some of the arrangements for Straight No Chaser to

perform at their gigs that summer. Rehearsals often happened at Dan's parents'
house, which had a nice piano and space for the guys to gather together and
practice. Walt would show up with staff paper and scratch out the arrangements
by hand. Anyone who was arranging music in the group would bring their
contributions, and they would learn the songs together. It was much easier to
make adjustments on the fly if they all practiced together. Walt would erase
notes, specific chords, or entire sections of a song that didn't work once he heard
it in person.

Arrange, rehearse, edit, perform, repeat. That summer took on its own
rhythm for Walt as he arranged more and more songs. The fifteen arrangements

MICHELADA

Cocktail

SERVES 2

This Mexican cocktail is likened to a Bloody Mary and is best made in pairs. Grab a buddy or serve yourself a double delight!

INGREDIENTS

1 lime, cut into wedges

Coarse salt

Chili powder

12 ounces clamato juice or tomato juice if preferred

¼ cup freshly squeezed lime juice, rinds reserved

1 tablespoon Worcestershire sauce

1 tablespoon soy sauce

2 teaspoons hot sauce

12-ounce can or bottle of light Mexican beer
   (Corona, Sol, Tecate, Modelo, etc.)

Rim your glasses by running a wedge of lime around the lip of the glass. Combine the coarse salt and chili powder on a small shallow plate, and dip or roll the lip of the glass into the mixture until coated.

Fill glasses with ice.

Starting with the clamato or tomato juice, split all ingredients evenly between the two glasses.

Finish by splitting the beer between the glasses, then garnish with a lime wedge and serve.

SNC High Note: This drink does not need to be well mixed when served. It's a spicy drink. Reduce the heat by limiting the chili powder on the rim and cutting the hot sauce in half.

Walt and Mike rehearsing their choreography for "The Christmas Can-Can" during sound check at Mystic Lake Casino in 2018. *Credit: Josh Adams*

he made that summer grew over the years as Straight No Chaser performed them in front of audiences. By the time they graduated, Straight No Chaser had more than one hundred songs in their repertoire.

The late 1990s were a good time for Walt to be curious about arranging music. The car break-in incident served a great purpose: it motivated Walt to find better, more efficient ways to create music and save it securely. After that summer's experience, he started learning Finale music software more seriously. He had some basic working knowledge of the program from high school. Like with most software, five years made an enormous difference in the technology. The clincher came Walt's junior year. Indiana University's Jacobs School of Music opened an advanced library equipped with dozens and dozens of iMac computers. This was a massive upgrade for Walt, who didn't have a personal computer at the time. Every chance he got, he would go to the School of Music and copy his arrangements to the software. Walt doesn't hide his type-A preferences, and seeing his arrangements clearly organized on the screen was exciting and gratifying. It inspired him to write more and get bolder with his arrangements. Technology made it easier for him to communicate with Straight No Chaser what he was hearing in his head.

Decades later, Walt's process for arranging a cappella–friendly music hasn't changed much since that senior year in college. He's more efficient. His ego doesn't get hurt as much when a song gets tossed aside. At his core, he's still the same as the nineteen-year-old in Chicago. He loves to experiment with songs. He gets excited at the potential of a new arrangement. He handwrites ideas on paper when they pop into his head. And he's still, above all, a cappella–friendly.

Crossovers

One of Walt's specialties is crossover arrangements. He loves to combine two songs that audiences don't anticipate hearing together. He may hear a single chord, recognize it in another song, and merge the two pieces

VEGETARIAN SAAG PANEER

Main Course (Vegetarian)

SERVES 5–6

Walt's most recent crossover was to eating a vegetarian diet. He still loves the occasional slab of ribs or homemade dish from his mom, but he gives dishes like saag paneer a run in his kitchen now.

PREP: 10 MINUTES   **COOK: 25 MINUTES**

INGREDIENTS

1 large onion, chopped

3 tablespoon grated fresh ginger

9 garlic cloves, minced

16 ounces fresh spinach

3 tablespoons vegetable oil

1 14-ounce package extra firm tofu, drained, pressed, and cut into 1-inch cubes

1 15-ounce can garbanzo beans, drained and rinsed

2 teaspoons ground turmeric

2 cup vegetable broth

2 tablespoons lemon juice

2 teaspoons ground cumin

2 teaspoons garam masala

2 teaspoons Asian chili paste

2 teaspoons granulated sugar

1 teaspoon salt

1 can 15-ounce full-fat coconut milk

Using a food processor, combine onion, ginger, garlic, and spinach; if you have too much spinach, do this in batches until spinach is very finely chopped.

Heat oil in a large skillet over medium-high heat; add tofu and cook for 10 minutes, until tofu cubes begin to brown lightly and crisp; toss tofu occasionally to cook on all sides.

Sprinkle turmeric over tofu and toss to coat.

Add spinach mixture, broth, lemon juice, cumin, garam masala, chili paste, sugar, and salt; stir to combine; reduce heat to medium and simmer for 10 minutes or until most liquids have cooked off.

Add coconut milk and cook for another minute.

Serve with rice.

SNC High Note: Press your tofu for about 20 minutes. If you haven't pressed tofu before, don't worry—there's a fun and easy trick to preparing tofu. Simply place tofu on several layers of paper towels, add more paper towels on top, and place a heavy cookbook, cutting board, or other weighted material to apply pressure and encourage moisture to drain from the tofu.

together in a crossover song that Straight No Chaser can add to their live show. Walt wants to make the audience forget that they're listening to a cappella entirely. Walt is extremely proud of the group's first onstage performance of a mash-up of Robin Thicke's "Blurred Lines" with Prince's "Kiss" getting a great reaction from the crowd.

Watching Straight No Chaser is not unlike watching your favorite sports team; each player is in the right position, making the right moves at the right time. Walt understands how important it is to give the audience the same kind of reason for loyalty as a sports team gives the fans in the stands. There's an unsaid commitment between the performers and the spectators. Fans promise to show up again and again if the performers deliver on the hope of something unexpected at every performance.

Walt is a living crossover between sports and entertainment. He is a lifelong sports fan and a loyal supporter of the Liverpool Football Club, the New York Mets, and the Philadelphia 76ers. He's obsessed with NBA culture, and he loves fantasy baseball. When his thoughts aren't occupied by his family or music arrangements, they're dominated by sports. Walt has been to twenty-five of the nation's thirty ballparks. When Walt's father died, his brothers-in-law made a commitment with Walt to travel to a ballpark every year to stay connected. The commitment to sports runs deep.

The connection between sports and music isn't hard to understand. Sports and music gather people together over a common experience and a shared enjoyment of a team or a group. Sports and music both draw on people's emotions. Walt still gets giddy with excitement thinking about his blitz trip with a friend to Madrid to see Liverpool FC win the UEFA Championship in 2019. From takeoff to return landing, Walt was gone for a total of forty-eight hours. Those two days were packed with quick cat naps in a hotel booked last-minute, the rush of the showdown between Tottenham and Liverpool, and victory celebrations.

That emotion as a spectator at a once-in-a-lifetime sports event rivals Walt's onstage feelings at once-in-a-lifetime performances with Straight No Chaser. The crossover between sports and music is so strong for Walt that he even hosted his own podcast called *The Chase Podcast* that covered sports and music. He stopped recording the podcast once he became a father. The 150-plus episodes featured guests like Sage Steele, co-host of ESPN's SportsCenter, and SNC alum

Ryan Ahlwardt, as they discussed music, sports, and more. Walt loves that music and sports both reflect the performers' preparation and precision in their skills. He hates that both have momentous events that end in just seconds, like a final homerun to win the World Series or a single-song performance at events like the Indy 500. It takes so much work to get to those moments, and they come and go in a flash.

The biggest difference between sports and music for Walt is that in music, there's no winner and loser. Straight No Chaser wants their audience to enjoy watching the shows as much as SNC enjoys performing them. To Walt, Straight No Chaser is the consistent winner because they all get to do what they love for a living. If they can create an experience for their audience that delivers emotions and helps create memories, they consider it a win.

The East Coast Gig and Donut Sign Debacle (Part Two)

No one can remember exactly what happened during the East Coast Gig Tour. Charlie's memory confidently places Jerome at the scene of the crime in Newburgh, New York. He recalls being between two high school gigs: they had finished the show at Patrick's high school and were on their way to Walt's high school to perform the second gig of the "tour." Walt's side of the story has the group returning from Boston University, where he recalls doing a small show, and on their way to Walt's high school in Pennsylvania. He places Steve at the scene of the crime alongside Charlie, and Jerome back in the getaway vehicle.

The details of the scene sound like they're coming from a bunch of college guys: a couple of semi-reliable narrators absolutely distracted by the action with very little commitment to the actual facts of the day. Because, in the end, the logistics didn't matter to the guys as much as the main event: they tried to pull a prank, which was actually a crime, and then managed to get away with some youthful defiance and a willingness to run fast before the cops arrived.

But the story didn't end with a clean getaway—everyone agrees on that detail. When we last left the guys in this story, half of Straight No Chaser was standing at Walt's high school. They were fresh off of canceling their gig for the students. They could only put off the school administrators for so long before they had to

BOSTON CREAM PIE

Dessert

SERVES 14–16

A dessert in honor of the East Coast Gig and Donut Sign Debacle. It's technically a cake, but cover-up stories are a theme here, so we're going with it.

PREP: 1 HOUR AND 10 MINUTES   COOK: 25 MINUTES

PASTRY CREAM

4 egg yolks

¾ cup granulated sugar

4 tablespoons cornstarch

2 cups milk

2 tablespoons salted butter

2 teaspoons vanilla extract

CAKE

2 ½ cups all-purpose flour

3 ½ teaspoons baking powder

½ teaspoon salt

**¾ cup unsalted butter,
   room temperature**

1 ½ cups sugar

3 tablespoons vegetable oil

1 tablespoon vanilla extract

4 large eggs

1 ¼ cups milk

CHOCOLATE GANACHE

1 cup semi-sweet chocolate chips

2 tablespoons corn syrup

½ cup heavy whipping cream

Preheat oven to 350°F.

Prepare the pastry cream by first beating egg yolks together in a medium mixing bowl and setting aside.

In a large saucepan, mix together sugar, cornstarch, and milk until smooth; cook over medium heat, stirring constantly, until mixture

begins to bubble, then simmer for 2 minutes and remove from heat.

Slowly add a small amount of the milk mixture to the mixing bowl with the egg yolks and whisk together.

Once combined, pour the egg mixture into the saucepan with the milk mixture and bring to a boil for 2 minutes, stirring constantly.

Remove from heat, add butter and vanilla extract, and stir until smooth.

Pour the mixture into a bowl and cover with plastic wrap; place in the refrigerator to cool.

Prepare the cake by lining the bottoms of two 9-inch cake pans with parchment paper and greasing the sides and edges.

In a medium mixing bowl, combine flour, baking powder, and salt; set aside.

Using a stand mixer, beat together butter, sugar, and oil and beat on medium speed until light and fluffy (about 4 minutes).

Add eggs and vanilla to the butter mixture and beat until fully incorporated.

Slowly add half of the dry ingredients and mix until mostly combined (not smooth).

Add the milk and mix until well combined; it may not appear smooth.

Add the remaining dry ingredients and mix until smooth; do not overmix.

Split the batter between the prepared cake pans; bake for 23–25 minutes.

Allow cakes to cool for 2–3 minutes before transferring to cooling racks.

Assess the evenness of your cake tops; if they have dome shapes, use a serrated knife to gently remove cake until the tops are flat.

Place one layer on a serving plate and top with pastry cream; then add second cake layer and set aside.

Prepare the chocolate ganache by combining the chocolate chips and corn syrup in a medium bowl.

In a saucepan, heat the whipping cream until it begins to boil; pour over chocolate chips and corn syrup; wait 2 minutes, then whisk together until smooth.

Pour the chocolate on top of the cake; start in the center and let the chocolate drop over the sides—this is part of the Boston Cream Pie experience!

Refrigerate cake until served.

SNC High Note: This is a crowd pleaser! The cake and the pastry cream can be prepared in advance, but the chocolate should be added within a couple of hours of serving so it can be fresh and the cake retains its sponginess.

claim a no-show and apologize profusely to the school. Charlie and his crew had started calling everyone they can think of to find the missing guys, unsure of what to do next.

Then, with a bit of bravado and some sheepish faces, the second half of Straight No Chaser rolls up to Walt's high school. Walt just missed his group's performance at his own high school. He apologized to the guys, explaining simply that they had to stop for some emergency repairs on Steve's car, which caused the delay. Everyone in Walt's car agreed: it was simply car trouble, and that's all.

Steve's car *did* have some issues when a radiator hose blew—but the issue was resolved rather quickly and the guys carried on. The *real* truth was that half of Straight No Chaser—Dan Ponce, Jerome, Walt, and DR—had spent the night in jail. On their way through Newburgh, New York, they had returned to the scene of the crime. In the cover of night, they stopped at the coffee shop again. The vinyl, rectangular "We Have Donuts" sign was still tethered to the sign holder, hardly impacted by Straight No Chaser's earlier attempt to steal it. It was just too tempting for Walt and the others to resist. They pulled over, cut down the sign, laughed like maniacs, and got back in the car to continue on their merry way. But just as they pulled out of the coffee shop, a cop pulled up directly behind them. They shoved the sign down on the floor of the back seat of the car as the cop came up to the window and peered inside, immediately seeing the sign crumpled on the floor of the backseat.

"Hey guys. Did you know that someone tried to steal that exact sign earlier today? They even had Indiana plates just like yours. What do you think about that?"

Just like that, Walt, Jerome, Dan and DR were on their way to jail. As the cops are doing intake paperwork, they ask for each guy's identification. The cops took their mugshots and fingerprints, and passed out a crunchy blanket and a flat pillow to each member and told them to get comfortable for the night. Walt was dying on the inside because he knew that literally no one in his life would be understanding of the fact that he got arrested. Not his parents, not his teachers, not his high school alma mater's administration, and definitely not Indiana University. The next day, the cops took the fully shackled Straight No Chaser members in front of the magistrate. Jerome had a cast on his wrist, so he was actually handcuffed *to* Dan. They each received a sentence of being on probation for six months in the state of New York. The booking cops sensed that the guys probably fell more in the camp of "terrible decision makers" more than "dangerous criminals," and they had a sense of humor about the incident. In fact, the police took a picture of the guys holding up the We Have Donuts sign and posed with the guys to commemorate the event.

After their sentencing, the guys wanted to rush to Walt's high school, but there was no way they could make it there in time. Collectively, Walt and his car full of lawbreakers agreed that it made the most sense to blame car troubles until further notice. That's exactly what they did.

Walt remembers finally cracking the story and telling the truth at the ICCA regional in St. Louis a week later. Holding the secret was just too much. The probation period was underway, and the guys were traveling as a group again. They were recounting stories and finally told the entire group the real reason they had missed the gig. They had returned to the scene of the earlier crime, found the sign, were caught by the police, and spent the night in jail. The other guys—the ones who had shown up for the gig but had been stood up by Steve's car—couldn't believe they had kept the truth to themselves. The group burst into laughter and had to hear the story all over again.

Walt's own secret lasted much longer. He didn't tell his mom the truth about that night, and the fact that he was on probation in New York for six months, until *eight years* later. Even then, telling his mom about his terrible decision as a teenager was an experience in humility and embarrassment.

Today, Walt, Charlie, and the rest of the guys still can't get the facts straight about that trip, but they all love telling the story. Perhaps they've replayed the events so many times that details get confused, or they've committed to not worrying about the details for the sake of a hilarious story. One way or another, the East Coast Gig Tour and the Donut Sign Debacle will live on in Straight No Chaser's shared memory as a night that no one will fully remember—and no one will forget.

(For the record, Charlie, Walt, and all of the other guys who shared their memory of this night made it clear that they don't condone their actions. But it did make for quite a story, and where else to tell a story but a cookbook! They're pretty sure everyone's moms know by now. If not, sorry, mom!)

Steve mid-dance during "Run Run Rudolph." When he decided to attend Indiana University, Steve's parents gave him sage advice: make the most of his time there. Now touring with many of his college friends, it seems Steve took that advice and ran with it.
Credit: Evan De Stefano Photography

VERSE 7

STEVE MORGAN

First, Scatter. Then, Reunite.

Steve Morgan doesn't try to hide his laughter when he thinks about the time when Straight No Chaser reunited for Mardi Gras in New Orleans. It was in 2002, the pocket of time after the original collegiate group had graduated and before they were picked up by Atlantic Records. In those years, Steve and the guys put in effort to stay connected to each other despite geographic distances and changing life circumstances. The getaway was promising from the start. DR, who worked for Hyatt at the time, had secured a room in the Hyatt overlooking Bourbon Street. Even the party they were invited to placed them on a balcony *directly* next door to the Playboy balcony—a logistical situation that no one complained about. That night, the guys hit the parties, ultimately losing one another in the drunken crowds and busy streets. They scattered: a couple of guys went one way, a couple of guys went another way. Occasionally, they would run back into each other, exchange stories of the night so far, and then disband again to follow the hope of more fun down the street. The next morning, there was a small group of Straight No Chaser guys who made it back to the Hyatt hotel rooms. The rest trickled in one by one. They nursed their hangovers, piecing the night together with hysterical laughter, stories, and—of course—a few musical

THE PRESBYTERIAN

Cocktail

This is the drink that you didn't know you were missing! This is a take on a recipe Steve's brother-in-law found one night, and it is fantastic. It's like a boozy ginger ale, but the rhubarb bitters impart a nice nuance, and the burned orange peel really changes the molecular structure of this drink (according to Steve, at least). It's really not the same without it!

INGREDIENTS

2 ounces bourbon
2 ounces ginger beer
Rhubarb bitters
1 orange twist

Fill a highball glass with ice.

Fill half the glass with bourbon, and then half the glass with ginger beer.

Add 4–5 dashes of rhubarb bitters.

Burn the orange peel, add to the drink and mix in vigorously.

You're welcome!

SNC High Note: A quick search online will get you all the right information on where to easily buy or how to make rhubarb bitters.

numbers dropped in for good measure. Some of the stories from that trip never made it out of the Hyatt, and Steve is definitely okay with that.

This process of scattering and reuniting on the streets of New Orleans was actually a telling sign for what was to come for Straight No Chaser in the following years. After the Mardi Gras debauchery, the guys returned to their homes across the country. They would come back together again for the next reunion. It felt to Steve that no time had passed at all when they reunited, regardless of how long it had actually been, since the group was all together. This ebbing and flowing of their friendships kept the guys connected without stress or pressure. They let their lives unfold with the knowledge that there was something really powerful about the group they formed together at Indiana University.

The reunions weren't always quite the Mardi Gras caliber. Often, they were better and more personally momentous occasions like weddings. In fact, when Steve and his wife, Emily, were planning their wedding, Steve's mother- and father-in-law were debating whether to have a DJ or a band at the reception. They hadn't known Steve during his time in Straight No Chaser's collegiate group, and the professional group hadn't taken off yet. Steve ensured his future in-laws that no matter which way they wanted to go, be it DJ or a band, they were guaranteed to have live music. At his rehearsal dinner, the Straight No Chaser members in attendance got up and sang a bit and much to the relief of his new family, they sounded good despite not having sung together for several years.

Even in those years after graduating from IU when there was no hint that Straight No Chaser would become a professional group, the guys would reunite and sing. It was lovely when it was from the heart. They sang "Ave Maria" at Dan Ponce's wedding and at Tyler's wedding, and also sang at Walt's wedding, and Mike Itkoff's, too. In Steve's opinion, it's an honor to be included in his friends' life events in such a special way. The sentimentality comes with the talent: it's a skill to be able to communicate feelings and emotions through song alongside close friends.

Sweet life moments account for a portion of Straight No Chaser's "in-the-wild" performances. Many, many others are peppered with hysterics and the goofy charm that entertain Chasers. Take, for instance, the night the Chicago

Bulls won the World Championship. It was 1998, and the guys were celebrating the victory at a bar. They were a few rounds into the night when one of the guys (the memories are hazy) spotted a woman at the bar that he wanted to impress. As if on cue, the buzzed Straight No Chaser aligned for an impromptu serenade —a classic a cappella move. They started, and it was *horrible*. Steve remembers the awkwardness of the whole group being completely off-key and out of time. The serenade was *not* working to the guys' advantage. Steve recalled one of the guys yelling "Abort Mission!" loud enough for them all to hear, and just like that, they stopped the serenade mid-song and vanished into the crowd.

Whether it's a night out on Bourbon Street or singing "Ave Maria" at a wedding, Straight No Chaser mastered a powerful tool when it comes to being a professional singing group: the ability to scatter and reunite without missing a beat in between.

Sorry About Your Forehead

Of all the things that Steve gets asked to autograph, he feels the worst about signing foreheads. After live performances, Straight No Chaser dedicates time to meeting with fans as often as they can. It's an opportunity to see loyal Chasers, catch up on their lives, and sign merchandise for new and longtime fans alike. Steve's used to some of the standard requests like signing t-shirts, albums, and photos. It's the foreheads that stand out. Don't get him wrong—Steve will gladly sign a forehead when given the opportunity. But there's something about the moment that the permanent marker meets the skin that just feels *wrong*. He gets flashes of the person waking up the next day, preparing to go to work, and regretting how they lost their sanity for a brief second in the meet and greet line. Steve signs anyway, but not without whispering, "Sorry about your forehead."

After a challenging 2020, Steve misses signing people's faces, merchandise, and—in the rare occasion—prosthetic limbs. It was the first year that Straight No Chaser had no notable in-person contact with fans due to the coronavirus pandemic. In a normal touring year, Steve and the other guys have lots of chances to chat with new fans and catch up with long-term Chasers. It's part of what he loves about touring. Seeing familiar faces pop up in the crowd with

PETER PIPER'S PICKLED PLATTER

Appetizer

SERVES 8–10

Steve and Emily found the inspiration for this dish at a little restaurant in northern Kentucky called Bouquet. Their chef was of the opinion that pickling was a great way to enhance and brighten the natural flavor of many things, and after trying this, the Morgans couldn't agree more. The platter had many different options, and Steve tried them all before settling on their favorite combination, which is what is featured below.

PREP: 25 MINUTES.

PREPARE IN ADVANCE: BEET PICKLED EGGS REQUIRE 48 HOURS.

COOK: 15 MINUTES

BEET PICKLED EGGS

8 hard-boiled eggs, peeled

2 15-ounce cans pickled beets; juices saved

1 onion, chopped

1 cup white sugar

¾ cup of cider vinegar

½ teaspoon salt

⅛ teaspoon black pepper

2 bay leaves

12 whole cloves

Place beets, onions, and eggs in a glass container.

In a saucepan, add sugar, 1 cup of canned beet juice, vinegar, salt, black pepper, bay leaves, and cloves and bring to a boil.

Once it boils, lower the heat, and simmer for 5 minutes.

Pour the liquid over the eggs, cover, and refrigerate 48 hours before serving.

PICKLED MUSTARD SEEDS

1 cup yellow mustard seeds

1 cup rice wine vinegar

¾ cup water

¾ cup mirin

½ cup granulated sugar

1 tablespoon kosher salt

—————————————

Combine all ingredients in a saucepan and bring to a gentle simmer over low heat.

Cook roughly an hour, until the seeds are plump. If too much liquid evaporates, add enough water to cover the seeds.

Cool and store in a glass jar in the refrigerator. It will last for 6–8 weeks.

GARLIC CROSTINI

1 baguette

Extra virgin olive oil

Fresh garlic cloves

—————————————

Cut ¼-inch slices of the baguette and place on a large baking sheet. Brush on olive oil.

Broil the bread for 2 minutes.

Cut the fresh garlic clove in half, and as soon as you take the bread out, brush the garlic on each piece of bread.

SNC High Note: And for the pièce de résistance, combine these elements for a glorious amuse-bouche! On the crostini, stack a pickled beet, next a slice of the egg, then a strip of the pickled onion, and top with a dollop of the mustard seeds. Sweet, savory, crunchy, juicy, and umami all in one!

a knowing smile is a comfort on long tours, and catching up with Chasers in the meet and greets often reignites energy that can be drained after an intense show.

The 2020 livestream concerts were a change from everything that Straight No Chaser and Chasers alike had come to anticipate from a tour. The live, onstage performances welcomed virtual guests only. Chasers streamed the concerts from the comfort and safety of their homes. Audience members could interact with one another through the show's chat function, which was streaming constantly during the performance. Although Steve and the guys could see the chat at a glance, there was no other way to really hear from the audience. The chat moved very rapidly as Chasers entered in their reactions to the show—comments would be gone from the screen as quickly as they arrived. Instead of relying on the chat to create an opportunity to connect with fans, Straight No Chaser offered online meet and greet events. Two hours before the show started, Steve and the rest of Straight No Chaser would take their seats on stage at the MGM Casino at National Harbor in Washington, DC. When they were settled, the virtual platform would bring onto the screen the first VIP guests for a chance to chat and hang with the guys. Chasers also had the option of requesting two songs for their own personal concert.

In this mid-pandemic world, Steve was grateful for the chance to see fans up close and personal, even if they couldn't give hugs, shake hands, or sign foreheads. In fact, it gave SNC the opportunity to meet Chasers in a quiet and focused setting. The virtual meet and greet events even had their own benefits that Steve hadn't anticipated. During one session, Straight No Chaser was delighted to see the Hurst family pop on screen. Steve recognized them as longtime fans, as he'd met the family, including their young twins, many times at concerts. The Hursts had a special guest with them—their new daughter, Violet, who was still very much a young baby at the time of the Meet & Greet. Steve and the rest of Straight No Chaser got to get all of their coos in over the newest Chaser on the screen, which is something that was only made possible through the virtual setting. Steve was thrilled to have the chance to "ooh" and "ahh" over Violet and be invited into the family's joy for a few minutes before that night's performance began.

Steve laughing with a Chaser during the signing line after a show. The fans keep the group energized and are easily the best part of touring. *Credit: Evan De Stefano Photography*

That feeling of family is not unique to Steve; all of Straight No Chaser refers to Chasers as part of their SNC family. Steve gives the Chasers credit for motivating the group to continue pushing forward and exploring new ways to cultivate the relationships they've created with fans over the past twenty-five years. Putting together the livestream shows was about upholding the traditions and celebrations that both SNC and Chasers look forward to each year. The virtual stage might not offer the same thrill of walking out onto the stage at Red Rocks or performing in the beautiful Espace Pierre Cardin in Paris. But at some point,

Straight No Chaser huddling before a performance, just before chanting "1, 2, 3. SNC!",
a college tradition the group has continued since they started touring.
Credit: Evan De Stefano Photography

the stage simply becomes the background. Straight No Chaser does holiday tours every year, and wanted to find a way to keep that tradition alive in 2020. This promise to fans is as important to Steve as any written contract with a record label. In many ways, the social contract provides even more in return. It gives SNC the opportunity to show up for the people who make it all possible: the fans. There are great venues and memorable shows. When the lights go down and a tour wraps, the moments that stick out the most are centered around people.

The Pipe Dream That Came to Be

1, 2, 3. SNC!

That's the chant that Straight No Chaser says together before every show. Steve is usually quiet before they take to the stage. He's rehearsing his remarks for the opening introduction. He writes a script out, aiming to get the audience engaged with the group from the start. Steve has learned over the years that he will get a laugh during his opening intro no matter what. He's usually aiming for that laugh to come from the audience. Sometimes, the jokes work and the audience rewards him with a laugh. When it doesn't, the guys in the group laugh at his flop. Either way, he's getting a laugh, and there's some security in that.

Twenty-five years later, there's actually quite a bit of security in Straight No Chaser. It doesn't come from the backup plan of getting a teasing laugh from the guys on stage. It doesn't come from the preshow huddle or the ritual of sharing show notes the day following a performance. The security comes from the fact that Straight No Chaser is a family.

The guys of Straight No Chaser talk about the family element in different ways. Some call it a fraternity. Others call it a brotherhood or a tradition. It's a legacy or an institution. The vocabulary might change from member to member, but it all gets to the same core meaning. There's a longstanding relationship between any individual member and Straight No Chaser that is hard to describe. Some of the members, like Steve, have

come and gone from the group over the years. New guys join when others decide it's the right time for them to retire from the Straight No Chaser life. At any given time, there are nine or ten active members. The Straight No Chaser family is much, much larger. It encompasses the original members, retired members, current singers, the collegiate group (now called Another Round), and each guy's own family.

The fact that Straight No Chaser has been around for twenty-five years means that the group has grown and changed as the SNC members have grown and changed. Steve was just a freshman in college when he auditioned for the original Straight No Chaser group. His life at eighteen years old looks completely

ARUGULA SALAD WITH AND SHAVED PARMESAN AND LILY'S DRESSING

Side Dish

SERVES 4

Steve's older child, Lily, has taken after Steve's skills in the kitchen. She will often pick up a cookbook and offer to cook for her family. One of her signature recipes is this dressing, which gets comments and compliments every time it's served.

PREP: 10 MINUTES   **COOK: <5 MINUTES**

SALAD

5 ounces baby arugula

Freshly grated Parmigiano-Reggiano (accept no substitutes!)

LILY'S DRESSING

4 ounces extra virgin olive oil

4 ounces apple cider vinegar

1 ½ teaspoon honey

1 tablespoon mustard (Dijon or stone ground)

2 teaspoons lime or lemon juice

¼ teaspoons black pepper

⅛ teaspoons salt

Top arugula with grated cheese and dress the salad immediately before serving.

SNC High Notes: **The leaves of arugula are very delicate, so you don't want them to get soggy. No one likes soggy anything.**

Steve belting the high notes during a show. What started in college as a reason to meet women and get free food, Steve says, has allowed him to grow together with his best friends, both on and off the stage. *Credit: Evan De Stefano Photography*

different from his life today. He's married, and he and his wife, Emily, have two children. Being a parent while working as a musician can be challenging for the guys. They work on tour and travel for months at a time.

Is this a viable career or a pipe dream?

The call from Atlantic Records was the first major indication that there was potential for Straight No Chaser to be a professional occupation. Steve was performing in *Mamma Mia!* on Broadway when the call from Dan Ponce and Randy Stine came through about the Atlantic Records meeting. At the time, Steve and Emily, also a performer, were married and discussing starting a family.

He was thinking about the need to have a "big boy job," in his words, to support his growing family. But he and Emily loved being performers, and they believed in Straight No Chaser. Steve took the leap with the other guys.

The first couple of years in any group can be a challenge, and this was true for Straight No Chaser. In the winter of 2008, Steve took two red-eyes home after shows to be back for grad school finals in Bloomington (not surprisingly, these did not go well). He loved being a part of Straight No Chaser, but he also saw that his family life was changing, too. He and Emily were expecting their first child and building a life together. The ups and downs of performance life meant some significant sacrifices for a family. Steve had some decisions to make. He spent Christmas Day that year sitting in the Cavaliers arena in Cleveland waiting to do the game-day performance. It was his last show before deciding it was time to step away from Straight No Chaser. It wasn't so much that Steve didn't believe in what was possible with the group. It was actually the opposite: he believed so fiercely that they were going to make it that he stepped back to make sure that was a possibility. At the time, Steve knew that he had one foot in other commitments in his life. The last thing he wanted was to hold the group back or make it complicated to move forward.

Steve's journey with Straight No Chaser may seem atypical to someone not in the entertainment industry. Within the group, it's exactly the right journey. The group grows and expands as each member's family changes and their personal lives call for more, or less, time for Straight No Chaser. That's the thing about Straight No Chaser being a family—there's no resentment when one member needs to adjust his life to make room for something different. Straight No Chaser isn't about one guy or one voice. It's a full family, and they put the needs of each individual first. SNC has your back.

Steve's story is even more proof of the brotherhood of the group. In 2013, another Straight No Chaser member, Ryan Ahlwardt, left the group for his own reasons. The group called Steve to see if his current life circumstances would allow him to go back on the road with the group. Steve had gone to graduate school and was working at a bank. Timing was everything. Using that math-loving brain of his, he and Emily made some calculations. They had had their daughter, Lily, and son, Will. The decision, this time, was pretty easy. It was time to become an active part of the Straight No Chaser family again.

ROASTED PEACHES WITH HOMEMADE CINNAMON WHIPPED CREAM

Dessert

SERVES 8

This recipe is inspired by a version Steve saw on the Emeril Lagasse cooking show (and yes, he knows that immediately ages him). The version is so simple but offers all of the delicious flavors of a perfect peach cobbler.

PREP: 5 MINUTES   **COOK: 40 MINUTES**

INGREDIENTS

8 peaches
Extra virgin olive oil
Sea salt or Kosher salt
1 pint whipping cream
1 tablespoon sugar
2 teaspoons cinnamon

Preheat oven to 350°F.

Slather peaches with olive oil and sprinkle with salt.

Roast for 40 minutes, or until the skin of the peach bursts from the fruit swelling so much.

In a stand mixer, beat the cream until it solidifies to form peaks.

Add sugar and cinnamon, and mix again until incorporated. Adjust the taste as desired.

Place a good dollop of the whipped cream in a bowl and top with a peach. Enjoy!

SNC High Note: **Double the amount of cinnamon whipped cream. In Steve's experience, small tastes from the cook and family members leave only half of the recipe by the time the dessert is served.**

And for a true Emeril touch, add a pinch of cayenne pepper to the whipped cinnamon to help bring out the cinnamon

Steve merged his two different lifestyles. One day, Straight No Chaser is selling thousands of concert tickets and selling out venues. The next day, Steve is picking up his share of household duties, vacuuming, and wiping down his children. And, of course, cooking up delicious meals.

The family balance is still interesting for most of the guys. A year like 2020 brought many things into perspective. Homelife ramped up for families across the country, and that included those of Straight No Chaser's members. For those of the guys with kids at home, fatherhood got a lot more hands-on. Randy welcomed a new baby to his family. Tyler got married. Steve was around for more ballet class drop-offs for Lily and soccer practice pickups for Will.

There will be more guys who leave the group as their family lives change and their professional ambitions shift direction. The members may come and go, but they share the thread of being a part of the Straight No Chaser family, now and always.

They Came. They Showed Us Up. They Took Our Women.

An honest answer about why many of the Straight No Chaser men joined the group was for attention and a social scene. In other words, attention from women. Indiana University draws a lot of students who have an affinity for music and performance. There was an energy to SNC that made them particularly popular. First, there was the rebellious name. Straight No Chaser, of course, has connotations of drinking. Indiana University was a dry campus so by name alone they were edgy. All of the original members were also part of the well-known co-ed campus group called the Singing Hoosiers. The subgroup of Straight No Chaser was, in many ways, like an exclusive club. But more than anything, the Straight No Chaser guys didn't act with the ego of a group that would one day get a record deal. They were just passionate, friendly guys who sang well and had a good time together.

The first big confidence boost came a couple of months after the group formed. The University of Illinois a cappella group, the Other Guys, called on Straight No Chaser to fill in a last-minute opening in their a cappella invitational. It was a beautiful Saturday morning, and the concert was taking place that night about three hours away from the Indiana University campus. The guys were living in a world before cell phones and text messages, and finding ten guys on a Saturday morning on any college campus is no small feat. Randy and Dan corralled the guys in the best way they knew how: a good, old-fashioned phone tree. In a matter of hours, all ten members of the group were gathered together. They knocked out a fire-drill planning session and rehearsal, then jumped in their cars to get to the show.

They arrived at the University of Illinois and delivered a performance that earned the only two standing ovations of the night. In the words of one of the Other Guys: "They came. They showed us up. They took our women."

Dominating the scene as new men on campus wasn't a one-time event for Straight No Chaser. One of Steve's favorite memories from the group happened early in Straight No Chaser's formation. They had been a group for only a year and a half when they decided to compete in the National Championship of Collegiate A Cappella (now known as the International Championship of Collegiate A Cappella or ICCAs). As a young group, the NCCAs were a big deal. It gathered all of the most elite a cappella groups from across the nation into a single championship. At the time, the Ivy League still ruled the a cappella scene. The Midwest simply wasn't a huge player when compared to the generational groups that existed at Yale, Princeton, and Harvard. Straight No Chaser had a few things going for them at the time: First, they were young and hungry to make a name for themselves. Second, they didn't have any alumni putting the intimidation of the championship in their head. They were fresh and wanted to compete. There were a series of regional events that had to be secured first before making it to the final round. Their drive, talent, and unique arrangements propelled the group through the regional events and all the way to the finals, held in New York City's Carnegie Hall.

Stepping onto the stage at Carnegie is still one of the most affecting moments that Steve can remember from his collegiate years. Straight No Chaser made a weekend out of the occasion. It was early spring, and they were excited to be in New York. On Friday, a handful of the guys went to see the Broadway musical *Titanic* and, on Sunday, went to see *Ragtime* on Forty-Second Street. But sandwiched in between, Steve and the other members took to the stage for the

NCCA finals. Straight No Chaser performed four songs, two of them original compositions, including a peer favorite, "Dry Campus." The song was originally about Indiana University, but in the competition set, Straight No Chaser adjusted the lyrics to include references to all of their competitors. It went absolutely as well as it could have gone in Steve's opinion. In the end, Straight No Chaser didn't win, and the championship title went to the long-established men's group from the University of California, Berkeley. Despite the final results, memories were made and the milestones had been met. In just their second year as a group, Straight No Chaser had established themselves as a true competitor in the collegiate a cappella scene, and the nation took note.

In his recollections of his vast and varied adventures with Straight No Chaser, Steve tends to punctuate periods of his memories as a performer with experiences as a passionate foodie. He remembers performing at *Christmas in Washington*, the beloved annual TNT special that aired for thirty-three consecutive years. At that event, Steve shook hands with musicians and performers that he looked up to and respected, like Kristen Chenoweth, Darius Rucker, and the Casting Crowns, before singing to an audience of some of the most senior political leaders in the nation. Then, with equal amounts of enthusiasm and description, Steve can vividly recount the amazing shawarma rotisseries that he loves to get at the Bucharest Grill in Detroit when he gets the chance. Or other favorites like the Artists Lounge in Milwaukee, Rendezvous Ribs in Memphis, and What the Pho in Denver. On the musical experiences, there's his audition with Straight No Chaser that took place in what was effectively a closet in the music school, and his final onstage collegiate performance on the IU Musical Arts Center (MAC) stage—the first non-IU music school performance to take place during the academic year in the history of the university.

In the past, it's true that the initial reason for joining Straight No Chaser may have involved the social scene. Over the years, it's evolved into so much more than that. The experiences were only just starting the day they rallied the guys from across campus to step into a last-minute vacancy in an a cappella concert three hours away. Since then, they've grown into men (arguably), friends, global food-tasters, cooks, husbands, and fathers. It's anyone's guess where it goes from here.

Seggie catching a glimpse of one of the group's opening videos that play just before the start of a show. *Credit: Evan De Stefano Photography*

SEGGIE ISHO

Little Seggie's Big Lie

Seggie Isho had to quit playing the trumpet because his family could no longer afford the instrument.

This was totally untrue. It was the best lie that Seggie could come up with to get out of playing trumpet. He was in the 8th grade, and he had been scheming for ways to quit playing the instrument. Seggie was good, but he'd reached the age when playing trumpet in the school band was no longer cool, and he wanted out of there. He told his band director, Mr. McLaughlin, in the saddest voice he could muster that he had to quit playing because his family could no longer afford to pay for the instrument. He told his lie, bowed his head, and walked away.

A few days later, Mr. McLaughlin called Seggie back to his office. Good news! The school wanted to support Seggie and his talent, so they had pulled funds together to pay for Seggie's trumpet. Seggie sat sheepishly in the office while Mr. McLaughlin called his unsuspecting, very surprised parents to share the news that they no longer had to worry about making payments on Seggie's trumpet. It was fully taken care of. Seggie knew instantly that his plan had backfired. His parents explained to Mr. McLaughlin that his generosity was appreciated but not necessary. There was, in fact, no financial reason that Seggie couldn't continue playing trumpet. Seggie hung his head. He and trumpet were definitely stuck together now. His parents insisted the school's generosity not be wasted. Mr. McLaughlin returned the trumpet and got the school's money back, and Seggie kept playing in the band.

Seggie picked up the trumpet in the 5th grade. He and all of his classmates were escorted to a room full of instruments and instructed to pick an instrument. Seggie wanted to be a drummer, just like his big brother, Danny. Seggie cooled on that idea when he realized that they don't actually give a drum set to 5th graders, instead they learn how to play on a rubber mat. He thought maybe the saxophone would be cool, but another student had already claimed it. His teacher, Mr. Milch, handed Seggie a trumpet and told him to pretend to spit into the mouthpiece. Seggie did it, and he was able to play a note. Mr. Milch insisted that this was his instrument. Not a lot of 5th graders can figure out how to make legitimate sounds come out of a trumpet. Seggie nailed it on the first try. Trumpet it was.

At every stage of Seggie's musical journey, a music teacher was there to guide him towards success. In kindergarten, Dr. Phillips first noticed that Seggie had a singing ability and encouraged his parents to keep him involved in music. In the 5th grade, Mr. Milch insisted that Seggie play the trumpet after noticing his natural skills with the instrument. It was Mr. McLaughlin who kept him on track and gave him the wisdom to embrace his interests, regardless of what other students thought was cool. Ms. Hindelang, his show choir director, noticed Seggie's performance ability and taught him how to turn it into a lifelong asset. Mr. Ensley helped him focus on his stage presence and professionalism, encouraging Seggie to learn how to respect the stage and engage the audience. And finally, in a last-round push before he left for Indiana University, a trifecta of teachers in his life—Mr. Milch, Mr. Gollon, and Mr. Thoma—came together and helped Seggie evolve into a true musician and thespian.

Seggie played the trumpet for years. Despite playing through his first couple of years in high school, he wasn't sure if he was actually any good at the instrument. Seggie had gone to school in a tight-knit community of people where everyone knew their role. The stars of the football team were also stars of the basketball team. The performers in the school choir were also the stars of the musicals. Everyone was happy and had their place in the school ecosystem. Seggie was a first chair trumpet player, and he'd gotten comfortable in that position. During his junior year of high school, Seggie's family moved out of the school district. His principal offered to let him finish out his high school career in his high school despite living in a different district. Seggie considered his options. He could stay where he was and *think* he was a good trumpet player, or he could switch to the much larger high school in his new school district and *know* for sure if he was as good as people told him. Seggie switched schools, and he confirmed the accolades. He wasn't just a big fish in the small pond of his previous school. He had real, raw talent, and a future as a musician was his for the taking.

During his youth, Seggie played trumpet in the University of Michigan honors orchestra and the Detroit Civic orchestra. He was being actively recruited to attend the University of Michigan and learn from his brass section mentor, Bill Campbell. But Seggie's new high school vice principal encouraged Seggie to explore his options, and he mentioned Indiana University. It intrigued Seggie. His parents took him to visit, and he took one lesson with American trumpeter and IU professor John Rommel. That lesson and a tour of campus was all Seggie needed to experience before deciding to attend Indiana University to study trumpet performance.

Seggie was so focused on his path to become a professional trumpeter that he didn't even know about Straight No Chaser until his sophomore year. Seggie's friend Jessi was the first person to mention it to Seggie. They were performing together in an off-campus musical, and she encouraged Seggie to make it to Straight No Chaser's last night of auditions. Seggie was doubtful that he would be interested, but Jessi promised that the SNC guys were just like him, which was, in Seggie's words, "normal bros who liked to sing." Seggie went, and he was the last guy to audition and the last guy to make it that round. He and fellow trumpet player Tyler Trepp joined the group at the same time, and they sang with Straight No Chaser until they graduated in 2005. During his time performing with Straight No Chaser, Seggie realized that he loved being a performer. The lights suddenly dimmed on being a lifelong trumpet player. Sitting in a bay to play the trumpet with a professional orchestra now seemed to be a mismatch for Seggie, who was drawn to the spotlight he enjoyed onstage with Straight No Chaser. He was a performer at heart, and no lie was going to get him out of this one.

PERSIAN ARANCINI

Side Dish

SERVES 6 (ABOUT 18 RICE BALLS TOTAL)

Seggie may not be the designated SNC Foodie like Steve, but he knows how to influence him! After Seggie gifted Steve a Middle Eastern cookbook, Steve adapted some of the recipes for his kids and came up with several winners, including this modified Persian arancini. The biryani spices are especially nice when paired with a Middle Eastern sauce called Jajek. The family's verdict: delicious!

PREP: 60 MINUTES (FOR EGGPLANT) + 20 MINUTES
COOK: 40 MINUTES + 2 HOURS COOLING TIME

INGREDIENTS

⅛ cup olive oil

1 diced onion

1 diced eggplant, peeled (after dicing, salt and let sit 1 hour)

14.5 ounce can garbanzo beans, drained and partially smashed

1 cup short grain brown rice

2 cups chicken stock

1 tablespoon black pepper

1 teaspoon ground cloves

1 teaspoon ground allspice

¼ teaspoon ground cardamom

Zest of 1 lime

½ cup grated, salty cheese (Parmesan, cotija, etc.)

3 cups canola oil

8 ounce feta cheese block, diced into ½-inch cubes

½ cup flour

1 cup panko bread crumbs

2 eggs for egg wash

INSTRUCTIONS

Sauté the onion for 4 minutes, then add the eggplant and continue cooking another 4 minutes.

Add the garbanzo beans and rice and stir, making sure they get toasted a bit in the olive oil.

Add the stock and spices, stirring everything together.

Cover and bring to a low boil, reduce to simmer and let cook 35–40 minutes.

Add cheese to achieve desired consistency at the end of cooking.

Remove from heat and refrigerate for at least 2 hours.

Once cooled, prepare to make the arancini by heating oil to 365°F.

Set up 3 bowls: 1 with flour, 1 with egg wash, 1 with panko crumbs.

Wrap the rice mix around the feta cheese, roll in flour, dunk in egg wash, and roll in panko crumbs.

Place in heated oil and cook until golden brown, about 3 minutes.

Let cool and enjoy with jajek.

JAJEK

1 cup Greek yogurt

1 cucumber, peeled and diced

1 tablespoon minced garlic

1 tablespoon chopped fresh mint

Salt to taste

In a small mixing bowl, add all ingredients and mix to thoroughly combine.

Serve right away or store in an airtight container in the refrigerator until ready to use.

SNC High Note: These can be served as an appetizer or side dish, and they also work as a kid's main meal. So many arancini, so many options!

Seggie during a 2019 performance in Champaign, Illinois. While the music is at the core of the group, Seggie admits his fortune of meeting his future wife through the group as well. *Credit: Evan De Stefano Photography*

The Full Freight

Sargon "Seggie" Isho grew up in Madison Heights, Detroit. It was an ideal community for Seggie and his family. He remembers it as a safe and friendly neighborhood of hardworking, primarily blue-collar families who worked hard to make a living. Madison Heights was close enough to Detroit to experience culture, and yet had enough industry to support the many families that came to the area to work in the automotive industry. Detroit and the surrounding communities held a lot of promise for families like the Ishos, who immigrated to the United States from Baghdad, Iraq. Each immigrant family's story is different, but one thing that remains the same is the importance of finding a community to call home. Seggie's family found this in Madison Heights.

Detroit has a large Middle Eastern population. In fact, the greater Detroit region has the largest population of Assyrian and Chaldean Americans in the United States. In the middle of the century, the American automotive industry peaked. Jobs were plentiful and the cost of living was reasonable. Its appeal reached the Isho family. Seggie's mom emigrated from Iraq to Detroit when she was ten years old. Her family was friendly with Seggie's father's family. When Seggie's father was twenty-two, he called on the family acquaintances for an immigration sponsorship. Seggie's father moved in with his mother's family to live while he worked at Ford. The families agreed that a marriage between the two families was a smart move, and his father and mother were arranged to be married. The union was happy, and just after Seggie's older brother was born, the family moved from Detroit to Madison Heights.

Seggie learned a lot from his parents. His father quit his job at Ford to build his own business as a Better Made distributor for businesses all around Detroit. His entrepreneurial spirit carried on to Seggie's brother, Danny, who is a successful businessman in his own right and owns more than a hundred cell phone stores across the country. His mother eventually went back to school, got her degree in accounting and accepted a job that led to upper management within the Social Security Administration. There was a mentality of hard work and dedication in his family that Seggie learned from an early age. Commitment to work was important, but commitment to family was everything.

Seggie left Detroit to pursue his passion for the trumpet at Indiana University. After he graduated from IU, he went even farther west to California. He enrolled in the University of Southern California—to get his graduate degree in trumpet performance. He loved his time in Straight No Chaser, but he knew that he had a potential future as a trumpeter, too. He was in his second year of graduate work when his brother called him. He was growing his business in Las Vegas, and he needed Seggie's help. That was all Seggie needed to hear. He quit school and headed to Vegas. Seggie loved every minute of his time working with his brother. They grew the business during the days and had an incredible social scene at night. Friends from all times of Seggie's life came to visit (*"It's easy to be popular when you live in Las Vegas"*). Seggie built relationships with people in the nightlife industry, and he loved to be able to give his friends and family the VIP treatment when they came to town.

The lifestyle was intense, but Seggie was ready for it. He worked during the day in the business, then would stay out at nightclubs until 3 a.m. Back to work in the morning, rinse, and repeat. It was fun and exciting. It was hard work, but he took pride in building something with his brother. Seggie was largely content with his life, except for this small, nagging feeling that he wasn't actually doing any of the professions that he set out to do. He wasn't performing—outside of the "host your friends to a night out in Vegas" routine—and he wasn't playing the trumpet. A call from Straight No Chaser in 2009 changed all of that. Mike Itkoff was leaving the group, and Seggie was invited to audition. Spoiler: he made the group.

Seggie continued to live in Vegas and traveled to wherever SNC needed him to be. In 2011, he packed up for a trip to Los Angeles to record with the group. He stayed with fellow SNC singer Mike Luginbill in LA. For reasons Seggie can't remember, the recording session in LA was canceled. But Seggie remembers something much more important happening that week in California: he found his future wife, Jamie.

Sitting on Mike's couch in West Hollywood, Seggie was scrolling through Facebook killing time. He noticed that a girl from his high school popped up on his feed, and she was in Los Angeles at the time, too. Seggie reached out to her to see if she was available to grab a drink with him. They went to the Sunset Trocadero Lounge. In the first five minutes, Jamie accidentally spilled a drink on Seggie. She felt horrible. Seggie felt amazing. He knew by her reaction that she was a good person, and he wanted to spend more time with her. He asked her to go out again the next night (dinner at KOI), and the next night (the Belmont), and the next night (Social Cantina), and the next night, too (the movies). For six straight nights, Jamie and Seggie had a blitz marathon of getting-to-know-yous, and it was the beginning of a life together.

The couple got married in 2014. Seggie joined Jamie in Los Angeles. As fun as it was in LA, Seggie knew that family was everything to him as a kid. He wanted to recreate that for his own children. Seggie was aware of the demands of travel

COUSCOUS SALAD

Side Dish

SERVES 8

This couscous salad is packed with fresh flavor and is often suggested for spring and summer meals. But we like to eat all year round, so we suggest adding 2–4 tablespoons of balsamic vinegar in the winter months to give the recipe more depth of flavor.

PREP: 10 MINUTES   **COOK: 10 MINUTES**

INGREDIENTS

1 ½ cups dried couscous

¼ cup extra virgin olive oil

1 teaspoon Dijon mustard

½ teaspoon honey

1 teaspoon lemon zest

3 tablespoons fresh squeezed lemon juice

½ teaspoon salt

¼ teaspoon freshly ground black pepper

1 medium cucumber, diced

1 large tomato, diced

½ cup coarsely chopped fresh herbs

¼ cup chopped walnuts, toasted

¼ cup golden raisins

Follow instructions to prepare couscous, then set aside.

In a large bowl, combine oil, mustard, honey, lemon zest, lemon juice, salt, and pepper and whisk together.

Add in the couscous and stir to combine.

Add in the cucumber, tomato, herbs, walnuts and raisins.

Mix well and serve immediately or let cool for at least one hour for a cold salad.

SNC High Note: You can add shredded or diced chicken to transform this side dish into a main meal.

on a family, and he wanted Jamie to have all of the support she needed if he was going to be away for tours and performances. He told Jamie that knowing a couple of friends here and there in LA wasn't going to cut it for him. When it came to his kids' family network, they were going to need the full support of the community back home. Seggie and Jamie moved back to their hometown. Today, they're raising the next generation of Ishos in the suburbs of Detroit, exactly as Seggie imagined it.

The Devolution of a Palate

The pull of family is strong in the Isho world. Seggie grew up surrounded by family. He likened Middle Eastern meals to scenes from *My Big Fat Greek Wedding* or any film featuring an authentic Italian family: lots of people, lots of activity, tons of food. Seggie spent time with his cousins every day. Sundays were spent in a consistent routine of church, brunch with his dad's family, play time, and dinner with his mom's family. Kids congregated in the basement while adults cooked and gathered upstairs. The meals were plentiful and massive, rich with traditional Middle Eastern dishes.

Seggie's mother and father both loved to prepare food. The rules of the house were to always make the bed and respect the chef. When his mom started working full time, she taught Seggie and Danny how to prepare decent, wholesome meals so they could feed themselves properly after school. Uncle Ben's rice was a tragedy in the Isho house. Rice was to be made the proper way or not at all. The standards were high for flavorful, fresh meals. It was no secret that Seggie loved his father's Middle Eastern biryani the most. Biryani requires a lot of prep work, and yet somehow his family members would always "happen to have" biryani prepared when Seggie stopped by. He didn't let it go to waste. As Seggie got older, he learned to appreciate the fullness of spices, how to add heat in the right ratios, and the importance of using fresh ingredients as much as possible.

At Indiana University, Seggie's palate took a nose dive right into ranch dressing. His palate devolved from full flavors and homemade meals to Big Mouth Subs and Pizza Express. It wasn't that Bloomington doesn't have great food options. It was just that Seggie was a student and hungry. He learned the college artform of dipping nearly everything in ranch dressing. His mother would send Seggie back to campus after a trip home with tons of food prepared. Seggie would freeze them and eat them when he wanted it, but when it was gone, it was back to dorm food.

Seggie is the first to admit he's not a great cook. He likes to cut corners, and the results usually speak for themselves. In his list of priorities, cooking continues to fall deeper and deeper down the line. For most of his life, trumpet was his main focus. Then performance took over, and Straight No Chaser has held that priority steady since he joined the professional group in 2009. He likens his exploration of new songs and new arrangements to be a bit like cooking off-recipe. You have to know the basics, but part of the art of performing is knowing when to break the rules if it's going to make a big impact on the audience.

Seggie spends a lot of time working on lyrics with Tyler for Straight No Chaser's medleys. The beauty of these arrangements is that he is building off the base of something the audience knows, and then they're going off-recipe with new lyrics and a twist of humor. Seggie and Tyler experiment with a lot of different lyrics and combinations before serving up an arrangement to the group. From there, they'll see which jokes land, what is a miss, and what doesn't work well onstage. Seggie digs deep into his roots to come up with the creative language for the medleys. He credits his third grade teacher, Mrs. Alexander, for teaching him the creative writing process. Seggie recalls being instructed weekly to write stories about what's happening in a Norman Rockwell painting for assignments. The task encouraged Seggie to put his imagination to work in a situation that wouldn't naturally call for creativity. Songs are created to be performed a certain way, and the artists take great pride in their work. Altering songs is tricky work, and adding humor and lyrics to an existing song can be a challenge. The words have to fit right, be clear to understand on a first listen, and keep the integrity of the song intact.

Seggie likes to think of writing new lyrics to songs as creating poetry. The words need to follow the pattern, rhythm, and beat of the song. Seggie writes each song as a poem first, then reads and re-reads it to find glitches in the beat. He'll substitute words, rearrange their order, and make notes where they'll have

ASSYRIAN BIRYANI

Main Course

SERVES 6–8

Assyrian biryani gets its name from the spice combination featured in Seggie's recipe below. Biryani dishes can feature a combination of many different meats, and is traditionally served with rice. Seggie's version saves time by using a rotisserie chicken, but freshly boiled and pulled chicken would be the authentic way to prepare.

PREP: 60 MINUTES   **COOK: 60 MINUTES**

INGREDIENTS

2 cups basmati rice

1 pound ground beef

1 cooked rotisserie chicken

4 large potatoes, peeled and cubed

1 teaspoon biryani spice

6 tablespoons vegetable oil, divided

Salt

Black Pepper

INSTRUCTIONS

Place rice in a strainer, rinse using cold water, and set aside.

Place ground beef in a mixing bowl. Add black pepper and salt to taste. Mix well and make nickel sized meatballs.

Spray the pan with oil and fry the meatballs until golden brown. Set aside.

Shred rotisserie chicken, add biryani spice, mix and set aside.

Heat 3 tablespoons of vegetable oil in a frying pan, and add cubed potatoes and fry until golden. Set aside.

Heat 3 tablespoons of vegetable oil in a saucepan and reduce the flame. Add rice, stirring occasionally. Add 3 cups of hot water and salt. Cover rice and boil on high heat for 3–5 minutes, reduce heat when rice comes to a full boil. Cook for 10–15 minutes. Remove cover and stir rice once. Cover and cook for an additional 5–10 minutes or until cooked. Turn off heat and let stand for 10 minutes.

Combine meatballs, shredded chicken, and potatoes in a large saucepan. Add more biryani spice to taste. Add rice and gently mix. Heat saucepan on low for 5 minutes.

Serve and enjoy!

SNC High Note: Top with a tablespoon of plain yogurt. For extra flavor, cook rice in chicken broth instead of water. Biryani spice can be found at any local Middle Eastern market.

Straight No Chaser rehearsing together at the beautiful IU Auditorium. The group tries to return to the Bloomington campus often not only for performances, but also for tour rehearsals and album recordings. *Credit: Evan De Stefano Photography*

to add extra beats or emphasize certain sounds. Then they add the music back in, layer on the choreography, and give it a test run on stage. Each song brings its own flavor to the stage, but one exceptional song can make the whole concert worthwhile.

Just a Swirl of Crown, Please

In March 2016, Straight No Chaser stepped on stage for their first Warsaw, Poland, performance. The crowd was typical for one of the early European concerts. There were about two hundred people, a decent size for a new tour stop. They were performing at Klub Stodoła, and the set started like most. The audience was seated, as usual, and Straight No Chaser took the stage. Song by song, the atmosphere in the club changed. The energy picked up as SNC got into their set. Normally, the guys will see some head bobbing and foot tapping. An extra energetic fan might stand up for a song or two, but most audience members stay seated for the duration of a concert. Not that night in Warsaw. A couple of rows stood up and started dancing. Then half the room was up and moving. By the end of the show, all two hundred people were on their feet, down at front of the stage. It was so energetic and fun, and Seggie can't remember doing another show quite like that one in 2016.

It's possible that evening's performance was spectacular. It's more likely that the audience was a fresh audience with no prior experience of a Straight No Chaser concert. Their first performance in a newly added city always brings some freshness with it: the audience doesn't have a preconceived idea of what a Straight No Chaser show is supposed to be like. They don't know that the audience usually sits. All they know is that there are ten guys singing, dancing, and happy to be there. So, their fans that night in Poland rocked out with them.

Performing in other countries brings some of its own unique challenges for SNC. In countries where English is not the national language, they have

to keep in mind what their audiences' experience is with the songs. The speed at which lyrics fly out of their mouths can be hard for even native speakers to keep up with, so Seggie and the guys often adjust the lyrics slightly when they assume that English is the second, third, or fourth language of the audience. Straight No Chaser has no doubt that the audiences can keep up, but they do recognize that jokes and humor are arguably the hardest parts of a language to translate. The adjustments to the songs are more of their own way to give themselves an edge during their performance. Straight No Chaser wants to make the best impression on their audience, and that sometimes means making sure their lyrics are going to carry over well and their jokes will land when appropriate.

GOLD RUSH
BY CROWN ROYAL

Cocktail

This Crown Royal original recipe honors the perfect past and present of Straight No Chaser: shots of Crown combined with the performance elixir of honey and lemon.

INGREDIENTS

1.5 ounce Crown Royal Fine De Luxe

.75 ounce honey syrup (equal parts honey and water)

.75 ounce lemon juice

1 dash bitters

1 twist of lemon

In a shaker with ice, add Crown Royal Blended Canadian Whisky, honey syrup, and lemon juice.

Shake and strain into an ice-filled rocks glass.

Top with a dash of bitter and garnish with a lemon twist.

SNC High Note: Having bitters on hand in your home bar is a sure way to look like a bartending professional.

Seggie holds up a perk of returning to the IU Bloomington campus often: attending IU basketball games at Assembly Hall. *Credit: Evan De Stefano Photography*

Seggie has great memories of performing overseas, and he loves adding new experiences when he travels. And, like most SNC alum, he has great memories of performing at sea, too. Seggie worked on a cruise ship for six months as a singer. He recalls some fun performances on the ship, of course. But he also remembers drinking Crown Royal whiskey like a sailor (*"Enough Crown Royal to fill Lake*

Superior"). It was quite a time to be alive, and Seggie knew it. He enjoyed his time at sea in the same way he enjoyed his first couple of years with the professional group: having an absolutely stellar time throwing back drinks with the guys.

Back in Seggie's day, every new member to the collegiate Straight No Chaser group received a shot glass. The guys[1] would do a shot of "something brown" (usually whiskey, but they weren't picky) before each show. It was always under the guise of professionalism. Whiskey can open up the voice and lubricate the vocal cords before a show. Sometimes it was one shot, sometimes it was more. Either way, it loosened up the guys to perform on stage a bit. Seggie always gave his best at their performances, but the shows did end up serving as an intermission to their social life. Before-show rituals rolled right into after-show rituals at the Crazy Horse, which rolled right into after-after-show rituals at house parties.

Seggie and some of the SNC guys attempted to keep the collegiate level of socialization alive in the professional group. They hadn't yet learned the rigors of a tour schedule and what it meant to do fifty-plus shows on a tour. They also hadn't yet learned the demands of parenthood, which will render anyone exhausted. Their first few stops on a tour, the guys would go out after a show, have some drinks together, and then show up at the stage call the next day ready to go. But unlike the audience in Warsaw that got more and more energetic with every song, Seggie and the guys realized that they weren't in the minor leagues anymore. Touring can be exhausting, and as soon as they realized that they weren't performing at their best by the end of a tour, they dropped the partying and late-night social scene.

These days, Seggie's pre-show ritual looks a bit different than the rough and ready rituals of his collegiate years. There's significantly more lemon and honey tea involved, and substantially less Crown Royal. When the Crown does make an appearance, it's not the straight-to-the-mouth shot style. It's just a swirl, sipped in a most gentleman-like fashion. Pinkies up!

---

1. Those of legal age, of course.

| 165 |

SEGGIE ISHO

Mike getting ready in the dressing room before a show. *Credit: Josh Adams*

VERSE 9

MIKE LUGINBILL

Duetting Milestones

Mike Luginbill and Ryan Ahlwardt have been on a similar journey since they met in junior high. They passed through each other's circles until high school, when they developed a friendship at Hamilton Southeastern High School on the outskirts of Indianapolis. Their lives have been intertwined in all the best ways for more than two decades. Looking back, their friendship seems like it was destined to happen. Mike is grateful that it did.

There are several recurring themes in the lives of the Straight No Chaser members. One of them is singing on cruise ships. Another is an ability to not take themselves too seriously. And yet another is a demonstrated passion for performance and music from a very young age. Mike checks the box on all three. It's fun to picture all of the grown men who don dapper suits and ties for Straight No Chaser performances running around as little tykes singing and performing for their families. But, they did, and Mike fits the mold. He was a musical kid, and his family were his biggest supporters. His grandmother was a worship leader at church. Mike sang in his youth group choir. In middle school he added choir to his musical resume, and he hasn't stopped adding musical milestones since.

Many of those milestones happened alongside Ryan. Their friendship really took off in high school. They were both into music, and Mike had visions of pursuing music as a career. Ryan was right there with him. Mike wanted to be a musician, and he started working more seriously towards that goal year after year. When Mike and Ryan were seniors, they drove down from Indianapolis together to try out for Straight No Chaser, and they both made the cut. They sang in the group all four years they were at Indiana University, and, in their spare time, they worked together to record their own album under the band name Small Town City. They recorded at Airtime Studios in Bloomington, and the album featured ten original songs and a cover of America's "Tin Man." It was their first musical partnership, but certainly not their last.

Their songwriting partnership solidified in the year after graduating from IU. Mike and Ryan decided to sing aboard cruise ships as their next music career milestone. Between performances, Mike doubled down on his future as a career musician. He wrote songs and played them on his guitar until his fingers were calloused. He and Ryan used their time on the ship to write, arrange, and experiment with new songs and sounds. They also planned for their next steps once they were back on solid land: they were going to form a band.

Mike and Ryan recruited SNC alum and keyboardist Nick Jaenicke to form Mitchell Street Band in Bloomington. Mike sang lead vocals in the five-man group, which performed across the Midwest for several years. Ultimately, the group decided to part ways, and Mike took the opportunity to meet some other milestones. He moved to Los Angeles, recorded his first solo album, and enrolled in the Musicians' Institute to study music production and audio engineering.

Mike's years in Los Angeles were an important part of his personal life as well as his professional career. He learned what it meant to be a struggling musician. He played shows to just twenty people at a time. It was truly the gig life: taking small bookings here and there to keep his music career alive while he developed his skills as a producer and audio engineer. Mike also met the woman that would eventually become his wife. He was committed to finding ways to pull his music career together. He knew it would happen, but he just couldn't see exactly how at the time. In 2008, those pieces fell into place when he was called to join the professional Straight No Chaser group. They needed two vocalists, and they chose Mike and Ryan. The band was truly getting back together.

2018 LA PHOTO SHOOT SALAD

Appetizer

SERVES 6

This salad has a lot of components to make, but the guys swear it's worth the while! Each of the following pieces come together in a salad that Steve first experienced during a break from a photo shoot in Los Angeles in 2018. Make each of the individual recipes below, then combine them for a five-star salad.

Using the recipes found below, prepare each of the salad components (Roasted Carrots, Baked Ricotta, Spicy Pumpkin Seeds, Crispy Kale, and Toasted Pecan Vinaigrette).

To prepare the salad, divide kale evenly among salad bowls. Pre-dress your kale leaves or allow guests to add dressing. Top with carrots, baked ricotta, pumpkin seeds. Serve and enjoy!

ROASTED CARROTS

PREP: 20 MINUTES   COOK: 30–40 MINUTES

2 tablespoons coriander seeds

2 tablespoons cumin seeds

3 pounds carrots, peeled and cut into 4-inch sticks about ½ inch thick

3 tablespoons butter, melted

8 garlic cloves, minced

1 teaspoon salt

½ teaspoon pepper

Preheat oven to 400°F.

Toast coriander and cumin seeds in a skillet over medium heat for about one minute; stir frequently to avoid burning. Remove from heat and let cool, then grind with a mortar and pestle or spice grinder until fine.

In a large bowl, mix carrots, butter, garlic, salt, pepper, and ground spices; toss until carrots are thoroughly coated.

Coat two baking sheets with cooking spray; spread carrots out evenly on baking sheets.

Roast 15–20 until carrots are lightly browned; remove from the oven to stir and rotate sheets.

Return sheets to oven and bake for 15–20 more minutes.

BAKED RICOTTA

PREP: 10 MINUTES   COOK: 25 MINUTES

Butter for the baking dish

15 ounces whole-milk ricotta

2 large eggs

3.5 ounces Parmigiano-
  Reggiano, grated

Salt and freshly ground black
  pepper, to taste

Preheat the oven to 400°F.

Prepare a 2-cup baking dish
by coating with butter.

Beat all the ingredients in a
bowl with a fork or a standing
mixer until well combined.

Spoon mixture into baking dish.

Bake for 25 minutes or until
surface is golden and puffed.

SPICED PUMPKIN SEEDS

PREP: 10 MINUTES   COOK: 45 MINUTES

2 cups raw pumpkin seeds

2 tablespoons canola oil

1 teaspoon Worcestershire sauce

⅛ teaspoon hot pepper sauce

½ teaspoon salt

½ teaspoon paprika

¼ teaspoon ground cumin

¼ teaspoon cayenne pepper

Preheat oven to 250°F.

In a medium mixing bowl, add pumpkin
seeds, oil, Worcestershire sauce, and hot
pepper sauce. Toss the pumpkin seeds
to coat them well with liquid ingredients.

Add the salt, paprika, cumin, and
cayenne and toss to coat.

Prepare a baking sheet by lining it
with foil and greasing the foil; spread
pumpkin seeds evenly on the sheet.

Bake uncovered for about 45 minutes.

Cool completely before serving; can
be stored in an airtight container.

CRISPY KALE

PREP: 15 MINUTES   COOK: 15 MINUTES

2 bunches curly kale
¼ cup olive oil
Kosher salt and freshly ground black pepper
Fleur de sel

Preheat oven to 350°F.

Prepare kale leaves by cutting off hard stems and tearing large leaves in half; then wash and dry kale leaves and place them in a large mixing bowl.

Add the oil, salt, and pepper to the bowl; mix until the leaves are fully coated.

Lay kale on baking sheets (you may need up to three different sheets or cook in batches); kale must have plenty of space, otherwise it will steam instead of getting crisp.

Roast for 15 minutes until crisp; sprinkle with fleur de sel.

Repeat until all kale is roasted.

TOASTED PECAN VINAIGRETTE

PREP: 5 MINUTES   COOK: 10 MINUTES

½ cup pecan halves
¼ cup white wine vinegar
2 tablespoons real maple syrup
2 tablespoons chopped shallot
¾ cup olive oil
½ cup vegetable broth

Preheat oven to 350°F.

Lay pecan pieces on cookie sheet evenly spaced; bake for 10 minutes, stirring occasionally, or until toasted and fragrant; allow to fully cool before chopping into pieces.

Using a food processor, add pecans, vinegar, syrup and shallots.

Slowly add in olive oil while blending until smooth; add vegetable broth as needed to thin the dressing.

Season with salt and pepper.

Refrigerate and store in a sealed container for up to three weeks.

SNC High Note: You can toast the pumpkin seeds, prepare the dressing, and roast the carrots in advance of serving this salad to save time on day-of prep. The ricotta is best served warm from the oven, and the kale leaves should be served right away.

Original Music and Making Things New Again

There's a hierarchy to feeling starstruck. It's easy to think that Straight No Chaser would become accustomed to the excitement of meeting celebrities and having once-in-a-lifetime collaborations. After all, some would consider Straight No Chaser guys celebrities in their own right, though the guys themselves would argue that point. In 2013, Mike got a double dose of close celebrity encounters that left him humbled, dazzled, and excited.

Adam Schlesinger was an American singer-songwriter best known for founding multiple successful music groups, including Fountains of Wayne, Ivy, and Tinted Window. He died in April 2020, and his death left an indelible mark on Straight No Chaser. In 2014, Adam and David Javerbaum wrote a comedic Christmas song for Straight No Chaser. It was a major event for the guys to have the honor of working with someone they respected deeply for his passion and success as a songwriter and performer. Mike was tapped to sing the solo on the track, and, he would be performing a portion of the song in a duet with actress/singer/songwriter Kristen Bell. Bell is a bona fide celebrity, known for her performances in over fifty features films, television shows, and Broadway performances. Mike was living his dream. He had done the work as a solo artist to develop his talent, and Straight No Chaser was providing him the opportunity of a lifetime.

The song "Text Me Merry Christmas" was a comical arrangement about the demise of communication in the mobile-dominated world. The song premiered on RyanSeacrest.com, and within three days, the YouTube video had amassed 1.7 million views. The collaboration was a success.

The success of "Text Me Merry Christmas" was a reminder to the members of Straight No Chaser to keep working at their skills and talents. There are always pieces of their performances, both as individuals and a group, that they want to finesse. They're aware of the threats that exist to a group like Straight No Chaser: become stale, not appealing to new audiences, or mismanaging the comings and goings of new members. They've learned how to take these threats and use them to their advantage.

Mike reads over music during a rehearsal on the IU Auditorium stage, March 4, 2020.
Credit: Evan De Stefano Photography

MORGAN MONKEY BREAD

Dessert

This special take on classic monkey bread includes the Morgan family's special touch: a small pinch of cayenne pepper to bring out the cinnamon flavor. Yes, that's right—cayenne pepper! Give it a try. You won't regret it.

PREP: 20 MINUTES   **COOK: 40 MINUTES**

INGREDIENTS

3 cans buttermilk biscuits
1 cup sugar
Pinch of cayenne pepper
2 teaspoons of cinnamon
2 sticks butter
½ cup brown sugar (light or dark)

Preheat the oven to 350°F.

Cut each biscuit into quarters (use all three cans).

In a small bowl, combine sugar, cayenne pepper, and cinnamon; pour into gallon-sized Ziploc bag.

Place all biscuit pieces into the bag and shake to coat each piece.

Once all biscuits have been coated, place the biscuits in a Bundt pan; space them so the pan is filled evenly.

In a small saucepan, melt butter and brown sugar; stir until it is a uniform consistency and color.

Pour the brown sugar mixture evenly over the biscuit pieces in the Bundt pan.

Bake for 30–40 minutes until the crust is dark brown; allow to cool for 15 minutes before flipping over and serving.

SNC High Note: This is a great kid-friendly addition to brunch.

Mike plays to the camera during a show. *Evan De Stefano Photography*

When one member moves on from Straight No Chaser, the remaining guys regroup, evaluating their overall sound and performances. It's their opportunity to pause, take a step back, and look at how they want to move forward. They move together, navigating the changes like a school of well-dressed, in-tune fish. The only direction is forward, and it's up to them how to make it happen.

Mike knows that each guy takes the future of the group very seriously, even though they don't take themselves too seriously. Mike pushes himself to take on new challenges, like the one he took when the group was recording *Under the Influence*. It was the professional group's fourth album, but it was the first album that Mike stepped up to support some of the musical arrangements. To date, Mike had limited experience actually creating arrangements for the group. He had worked on his own music, but this time it was more than his own name on the line. He was thinking about the Straight No Chaser entity and wanted to do right by them.

Mike knew how he wanted some of the songs to sound, but he wasn't exactly sure how to get them there. His first arrangements were "Somebody That I Used to Know" and "Rolling in the Deep." He partnered with Seggie and Ryan to write the song "Everyday," the first non-holiday original song the professional Straight No Chaser group would release up to that point. Each song was a chance for Mike to learn more and find his own process. Each night that he stayed up late working on the arrangements moved him closer to a song that he was excited to present to the group. The rest of the group gave feedback and helped him hear things that he hadn't noticed on his own, and by the time the album was finished, Mike was ready to take on more.

One of the Lucky Ones

Yogi was a Straight No Chaser icon. Mike's fifteen-year-old Australian shepherd/ border collie was part of the Straight No Chaser family for his entire life and the entire life of the group's professional career. Yogi had been on tours and tour buses, in recording studios, and made friends with

OVEN-BRAISED SHORT RIBS WITH BLACK PEPPER AND CHIANTI

Main Course

SERVES 4–6

Honestly, who doesn't like a recipe that includes wine in the ingredients? We highly recommend sipping the rest of the Chianti while the ribs are roasting.

PREP: 15 MINUTES   **COOK: 4 HOURS**

INGREDIENTS

4 lbs. short ribs

1 tablespoon + 1 teaspoon salt

1 ¼ cups dry red wine (Chianti)

1 ¼ cups beef stock or broth

1 ¼ cups water

1 tablespoon tomato paste (a generous tablespoon)

Cloves of 1 large head of garlic, peeled

2 teaspoons fresh ground black pepper

4 large slices country-style bread

Olive oil

INSTRUCTIONS

Preheat oven to 350°F.

Set short ribs out of the refrigerator 30 minutes before starting to bring them to room temperature; salt liberally.

In a Dutch oven, bring wine, stock, and water to a boil, then reduce heat to medium and simmer for 3 minutes.

Add tomato paste to Dutch oven and dissolve. Set aside 1 garlic clove and add the rest to sauce with 1 tablespoon pepper. Add the meat to the Dutch oven.

Place the lid on the Dutch oven and bring to a low boil. Transfer to the preheated oven for 20 minutes, then reduce the heat to 250°F for 2.5–3 hours.

Remove Dutch oven from the oven, and remove the short ribs from the Dutch oven. Set the meat aside and tent with aluminum foil. Place the sauce back on the stove and bring to a steady boil for 15–30 minutes, reducing by half.

While the sauce is boiling, set the oven to broil. Drizzle olive oil on the bread, and broil for roughly 2 minutes until it browns. Remove from the boil and rub each piece with reserved garlic clove.

Add the remaining 1 teaspoon pepper to the meat. Reduce the sauce to a low simmer and add the meat back in.

Serve the short ribs in a low bowl and top with sauce and a slice of bread.

Save those bones and make a rocking' homemade bone broth! (But that's a recipe for another time . . .)

SNC High Note: Your guests likely won't care if these short ribs are served in a low bowl, but if you're looking for that chef's kiss, the bowl is it!

Chasers across the country. Mike and his wife, Zoë, got Yogi at the beginning of their relationship. It was a big move for the couple. Then again, most of Mike and Zoë's relationship was big moves.

The two met in Bloomington in 2006 through a winding series of mutual friends. Mike had returned from doing the cruise ship life, and he was performing with Mitchell Street Band. Zoë was in town visiting a friend. She had traveled from Texas and was planning to stay for the week. Mike met Zoë at the beginning of her visit, and they hung out for a large portion of her time in Bloomington. Three weeks after Zoë went back to Austin, Mike took a trip to visit her. Even in the early stages, they knew what they had was a big deal. They decided to date long distance, and Mike never looked back.

He considers himself one of the lucky ones. A big part of that reason is because of Zoë, whom he married in 2014. They have two daughters together and, of course, they had Yogi until he passed in August 2020. But all of Mike's experiences outside of Straight No Chaser have given him the priceless lesson of perspective. Prior to Straight No Chaser, Mike knows how rare it is to have a family that was as willing to commit to his dreams as he was. He never remembers his parents faltering in their support of his desire to become a professional musician. He credits his family for helping him through some of the initial hurdles of chasing his career and is eternally grateful for their willingness to support him in any way they could.

Like all of the guys, Mike understands the incredible opportunity he has to build his career as part of Straight No Chaser. SNC is never about one guy or one opportunity, but it does have the potential to change each member's individual life. As musicians, they can all leverage the collective experience as a group. After Zoë and Mike moved from Los Angeles to Nashville in 2014, Mike witnessed what a parallel path for him might have been had he not received the call from Straight No Chaser.

Nashville is called a "twelve-year town" by people in the music industry. It means that Nashville, barring the few exceptions, is a difficult place to find a break as a musician immediately upon arrival. In the years that Mike has lived there, he witnessed a lot of very talented people trying to make their way as professionals. Musicians flock to Nashville, and Mike is right in the center of the scene. During down time between tours and recording sessions, Mike likes to tap into his solo career. It's not consistent, and he does less solo music, particularly

GRAPEFRUIT JALAPENO CILANTRO SHRUB

Cocktail

As the SNC Foodie, Steve continues to be over-the-top when it comes to trying new recipes and combinations. He explored the world of shrubs and was hooked. This spicy-citrus blend sits for three days to let the flavors combine.

SHRUB

1 grapefruit, peeled and broken into small sections

1 jalapeno, sliced

1 handful cilantro

⅔ cup sugar

⅔ cup vinegar

Add all ingredients to a mason jar; shake vigorously and let sit for three days.

COCKTAIL

3 ounces shrub

2 ounces tequila

1 ounce sparkling water

Add ice to a highball glass.

Pour in tequila and shrub.

Top with sparkling water, swirl, and enjoy.

SNC High Note: When preparing the shrub, remove as much fibrous material from the grapefruit pieces as possible. For the heat, include the jalapeno seeds for more heat, remove them for less. Shrubs can be stored in airtight containers for up to two weeks.

now that he's a father and time feels fleeting. He focuses on writing and building a reputation as a songwriter. He knows he's worked hard, but he can't say for certain that he's worked any harder than the hundreds of other musicians he sees performing gigs in Nashville, hoping to be found. Everyone is good in Nashville, and so many musicians don't make it to the light of day. Sometimes, it's hard to watch, as Mike knows in his core that Straight No Chaser has made all the difference in his professional life.

The Scary Solo Career of a Soloist

There's a fun irony to Mike's experiences as a soloist. Singing solos has been Mike's comfort zone for years; with the onstage presence of the rest of the group, filling in the solos feels like home.

The longer Mike does solos within Straight No Chaser, the harder it becomes to do any solo performances outside of the group. Despite his comfort with performing multiple solo performances within a single Straight No Chaser concert—and several years as a solo artist—Mike sometimes finds it daunting to walk onto stage and perform without his SNC brotherhood up there with him. However, every now and again there are random opportunities for Mike to perform by himself.

Mike was feeling all of those things in April 2019 during the Charleston Songwriter Festival. Straight No Chaser's management group was hosting the three-day festival. It was the first time in a couple of years that Mike was going to be performing without the group, but it made sense for him to participate in the festival as a solo artist. It was one thing for Mike to perform on his own; it was something else to perform his own music in front of an audience of celebrated songwriters. He wrote three new songs and visited several of his older songs for the festival and delivered them to a packed crowd at the Republic Garden & Lounge. Although he was there as a solo artist, Mike realized that his audience included several Chasers, too—a testament to their commitment to supporting the group as well as individual members.

The Charleston Songwriter Festival was a great way for Mike to network with people in the music industry. Making meaningful connections can be a challenge as a full Straight No Chaser touring schedule will take them away from home for six months out of the year. It's part of the reason that Mike and Zoë ended up moving to Nashville. Mike joined the professional group in 2008. At the time, he and Zoë were living in Los Angeles, where rent and the cost of living were high. Mike is originally from Indiana, and Zoë is from Texas. They wanted to be somewhere between their families, and ideally in a city that could serve Zoë's career as a lawyer as well as Mike's career as a musician. Nashville made sense. It's the mecca of the music world for rising musicians and a city that many bands like to call home.

Being on tour presents some challenges to networking in the music industry back home, but it is essential to building relationships within the Straight No Chaser community. Mike finds touring to be the best way to connect with fans in real ways. He loves the chance to talk with people who come to the shows, hear their stories, and thank them for supporting the group. Tours are fast-paced and usually keep the guys moving on from location to location at a quick clip. Any chance to create quality interactions with fans is welcome, and Straight No Chaser has been creative over the years. In 2012, the group hosted the Chasers at Sea Carnival Cruise. It was a five-day, four-night cruise featuring Straight No Chaser as the main attraction. All day, every day, Chasers could have one-on-one interactions with their fans in ways that are completely different from standard tour events. There were no signing items at the merchandise table or grabbing pictures as the group made their way through the crowds. No, this was a different experience all together. Walt and Don hosted a scotch tasting, and DR did a wine tasting. The shows were as dynamic as the individual performances, and it was one of the first occasions where Chasers were able to experience some of the guys' other talents that don't make it to the stage during SNC performances. Jerome and Mike performed some of the songs that they had written together, and Mike added several of his solo songs, too. Seggie hit the stage with his trumpet, and Tyler played the piano.

The result was exactly what the group wanted it to be. A chance for the guys to be themselves, and for Chasers to have a chance to see each member as his own person. From Mike's perspective, having nine phenomenal performers on stage is an overwhelming advantage to Straight No Chaser. The group uses their individual personalities, humor, and skills to make the show better for everyone. Mike hopes that he has the privilege of singing with Straight No Chaser for a long, long time to come.

Straight No Chaser takes a photo with the audience during a show in Bloomington, Indiana. In 2010 the group began taking photos of the audience, and eventually it evolved that the guys would jump into the frames as well. The photos are shared on Facebook so fans can tag themselves in the fun. *Credit: Evan De Stefano Photography*

SOUNDING OFF

There is a symmetry between music and cooking. They both gather people together over a shared experience, engage multiple senses, and serve as a form of expression for the creators. The intent of this cookbook was to give you the opportunity to get to know each member of Straight No Chaser through insights and stories—stories that might be told over a meal.

Straight No Chaser is not so different from a great recipe: the whole is greater than the sum of the parts. The particular combination of nine personalities and voices creates an onstage result greater than any one member could produce on their own. In the group, like in a recipe, there is change and evolution over time, all while keeping the same goal of creating an enjoyable experience for the senses.

In the end, Straight No Chaser owes both our initial success and our longevity to the Chasers. Without their support, whether simply supporting the albums, showing up for shows, or actively spreading the word to others, the group wouldn't still be going strong at the twenty-five year mark. A sincere thanks to you for supporting Straight No Chaser over the years and bringing the group into your home in a new way through *Sound Bites*. Here's to gathering together with friends and loved ones to enjoy music, smooth drinks, and delicious food!